Biblical Lessons For The Heart

By Dr. Cynthia Owens K. Brown

Biblical lessons for The Heart © 2019 by Dr. Cynthia Owens K. Brown. All Rights Reserved. All rights reserved. No part of this book may be reproduced in any form or by any electronic or mechanical means including information storage and retrieval systems, without permission in writing from the author. The only exception is by a reviewer, who may quote short excerpts in a review.

Cover designed by Ayesha Andrews and Dylan Kiner

Dr. Cynthia Owens K. Brown
Visit my website at https://drcynthiakbrown.org

Printed in the United States of America

First Printing: Feb. 2020
Kindle Digital Publishing

Dedication

To my mom, Florence P. Owens, and to my children Dylan, Ayesha, Akilah, and Ashani, whose love and encouragement helped me to understand the potential benefits that might be derived by others through the publishing of these lessons. Special thanks to Dylan and Ayesha for their technical support in producing this book.

I especially thank Ayesha and Dylan for the beautiful cover that they designed. Finally, to my dear friend, Lavinia Walker, thank you for your love and encouragement, and for your valued support in the editing of these lessons.

PREFACE

Bible Lessons and Sermons for the Heart is a compilation of some of the lessons and sermons that were taught and preached by me over my twenty-five years of being a pastor in the City of Camden, New Jersey, a presiding elder of four churches, and a general elder over three churches. God gave each lesson to me in response to my prayer for a message that would benefit the hearers of that particular word.

All scriptures that are referenced in this book are taken from the King James Version of the Bible. All pronouns that reference the God of Abraham, Isaac, and Jacob; Christ Jesus; and the Holy Ghost, however, are capitalized by me in reverential honor of my triune God.

I have always written my lessons and sermons for presentation, even though I was not bound to read them verbatim. I can truly say that each one of these lessons and sermons has been a blessing to those who heard them. How can I be sure? I am sure, because at the time of their delivery, at least one hearer has said, "That lesson, or message, was for me. I needed to hear it." It has been my practice prior to preparing a message to ask the Lord God to please give me a message that will be a help to those who would hear it. Over the years, I have accumulated hundreds of lessons and sermons. My children, and others, continually suggested to me that these are worthy of my putting them in a book. It is my prayer that many will be encouraged, reassured, comforted, strengthened, corrected, and enlightened by the contents of each.

And, so, here it is. I pray that all who read this book will find answers to questions that have perplexed them; that each lesson will minister to a current need; and that the hearts of the readers will be pricked with a desire to yield to the Holy Spirit and to know more about Jesus and His Word.

TABLE OF CONTENTS

Lesson number One	"THANK GOD FOR THE BLOOD OF JESUS"	1
Lesson number Two	"A PROFITABLE RETURN ON YOUR INVESTMENT"	3
Lesson number Three	"BENEFITS OF FEARING GOD"	5
Lesson number Four	"STAND STILL AND SEE"	7
Lesson number Five	"DO NOT BE A TARGET FOR THE ENEMY?"	9
Lesson number Six	"A PICTURE OF A BALANCED LIFE IN CHRIST JESUS"	11
Lesson number Seven	"CURVE BALLS OF LIFE ARE NOT STRIKE OUTS"	13
Lesson number Eight	"PRAY: GOD ALWAYS ANSWERS PRAYER"	15
Lesson number Nine	"HAVE YOU RECEIVED THE HOLY GHOST SINCE YOU BELIEVED?"	17
Lesson number Ten	"MADE IN GOD'S IMAGE AND LIKENESS"	19
Lesson number Eleven	"THE UNIQUENESS OF JESUS"	21
Lesson number Twelve	"JESUS LOVES US"	23
Lesson number Thirteen	"JESUS: THE WAY, THE TRUTH, AND THE LIFE"	25
Lesson number Fourteen	"MORE THAN A PROPHET AND TEACHER: JESUS IS LORD"	27
Lesson number Fifteen	"KEEP YOUR GIFTS: JUST DO WHAT GOD SAYS"	29
Lesson number Sixteen	"OUR GOD IS FAITHFUL: NO NEED TO COMPROMISE"	31
Lesson number Seventeen	"LOVING JESUS IS MORE THAN A PROFESSION"	33
Lesson number Eighteen	"GOD IS NO RESPECTER OF PERSONS"	35
Lesson number Nineteen	"NO WEAPON FORMED AGAINST US SHALL PROSPER"	37
Lesson number Twenty	"THE PRISON OF AN UNFORGIVING MINDSET"	39
Lesson number Twenty-One	"THE BIBLE: THE STANDARD FOR RIGHTEOUS LIVING"	41
Lesson number Twenty-Two	"THE POWER OF THE BLOOD OF JESUS"	43
Lesson number Twenty-Three	"THERE IS LIFE AFTER THE STORM"	45
Lesson number Twenty-Four	"THIS IS JUST FOR A SEASON"	47
Lesson number Twenty-Five	"UNDERSTANDING THE TIMES: WE NEED JESUS"	49
Lesson number Twenty-Six	"WHEN YOU PRAY"	51
Lesson number Twenty-Seven	"WE CAN'T HURRY GOD"	53
Lesson number Twenty-Eight	"BE STEADY IN THIS UNSTEADY WORLD"	55
Lesson number Twenty-Nine	"FAITH THAT WORKS"	57
Lesson number Thirty	"TOMORROW MIGHT BE TOO LATE"	59
Lesson number Thirty-One	"I WILL BE CONTENT"	61
Lesson number Thirty-One	"BY ONE MAN"	63
Lesson number Thirty-One	"RESTORE ME"	65
Lesson number Thirty-One	"GET ANCHORED IN THE TRUTH AND STAND ON HIM"	67
Lesson number Thirty-One	"LIFE THROUGH GOD'S EYES"	69
Lesson number Thirty-One	"MISPLACED AFFECTION"	71
Lesson number Thirty-One	"OUR WORDS MATTER"	73
Lesson number Thirty-One	"A GRATEFUL HEART"	75
Lesson number Thirty-One	"LORD, HELP US TO STAND"	77
Lesson number Forty	"JESUS: THE BELIEVER'S ROLE MODEL"	79
Lesson number Forty-One	"GOD DELIGHTS IN OBEDIENCE"	81
Lesson number Forty-Two	"THE JOB MENTALITY"	83
Lesson number Forty-Three	"FAITH THAT IS REAL: DO YOU HAVE IT?"	85

INTRODUCTION

Some of life's experiences are unexpected, and we struggle to successfully cope with them, while carrying on our daily tasks. The biblical lessons in this book helped me to stay focused and grounded throughout many situations. And, because "The thing that hath been, it is that which shall be; and that which is done is that which shall be done: and there is no new thing under the sun," according to King Solomon, the writer of the book called Ecclesiastes, chapter 1, verse 9, it is quite likely that you, too, will have similar challenges and experiences in your life.

These lessons represent my heart's reflections and study on the topics given to me by God over thirty-three years of preaching and teaching His Word, and serving twenty-five of these years as a senior pastor. Many recipients of these teachings professed that the lessons were very timely in assisting them in dealing with situations that were current in their lives. In them, they found comfort, strength, hope, knowledge, and understanding. Therefore, it is my hope and sincere belief that you, too, will find these lessons to be timely words that minister to your hearts and to your situations. Read, study, and meditate on them, and ask God to "Open thou mine eyes, that I may behold wondrous things out of thy law." (Psalm 119:18) And, know that God will do it!

Lesson Number One

"Thank God For The Blood Of Jesus"

Text: **Hebrews 10:19-22** – "Having therefore, brethren, boldness to enter into the holiest by the blood of Jesus, by a new and living way, which He hath consecrated for us, through the veil, that is to say, His flesh; and having an High Priest over the house of God; let us draw near with a true heart in full assurance of faith, having our hearts sprinkled from an evil conscience, and our bodies washed with pure water."

INTRODUCTION

It has been said that Christianity is a very bloody religion. Everything seems to be about the blood. Most of the songs we sing are about the blood. Many of our personal testimonies are about the blood of Jesus. Even Jesus, Himself, suffered a bloody and horrific death on the cross. Though all of these are true, it is the significance of the blood that Christians celebrate. The Word of God tells us in Leviticus 17:11 that "… The life of the flesh is in the blood: and I have given it to you upon the altar to make an atonement for your souls: for it is the blood that maketh an atonement for the soul."

Prior to the coming of Jesus, God used a system of animal sacrifices for the atonement of the souls of humankind. This system was temporary, however, for it had to be performed by the High Priest every year on behalf of God's chosen people. And while the killing and presentation of the animal sacrifice unto God was a bloody process, its purpose and significance was reflective of that which God would eventually accomplish upon the cross through the killing and presentation of His only begotten son, Jesus, the Christ.

DISCUSSION

Under the previous system of atonement, God chose the tribe of Levi, specifically Aaron and his descendants, to be His priests before the people. They cared for the temple, and they were in charge of all that pertained to worship in the Temple. Inside the Temple, there was a veil that separated the High Priest and the people from the spiritual presence of God. That section of the temple was called the Holy of Holies.

The High Priest prepared himself to enter the Holy of Holies by five times washing his whole body, and by ten times washing his hands and his feet. He was allowed to enter that area of the Temple only once a year on the Day of Atonement, which is also called "Yom Kippur" in the Hebrew language. On this day, the High Priest offered a blood sacrifice for the forgiveness of his sins, his family's sins, and for the sins of all of the people of God. This day was the 10th day of the 7th month, which was Tishri on the Hebrew calendar, according to the movement of both the Lunar and Solar systems, and September, or early October on our Gregorian calendar system.

On the Day of Atonement a goat was chosen, a red scarlet cloth was tied to its horn, and the goat was placed before the people, as they cast their sins upon it. The High Priest would then go in and out of the Holy of Holies to perform various rituals of offerings and sacrifices, and to sprinkle blood on the mercy seat towards the veil and altar of incense. This system was a shadow of that which was to come, because the blood of goats and calves could not eternally wash away the sins of humankind. Therefore, God sent His only begotten Son into the world to be the final sacrifice for sin. This act reflected God's love for humankind, as recorded in the third chapter of the Gospel of John, verse sixteen, which states, "For God so loved the world, that He gave His only begotten Son, that whosoever believeth in Him should not perish, but have everlasting life." And, just as the people in the former system of redemption cast their sins upon the scape goat, God "...Hath made Him [His Son] to be sin for us, who knew no sin; that we might be made the righteousness of God in Him," (2 Corinthians 5:21), for "...by His own blood He entered in once into the holy place, having obtained eternal redemption for us." (Hebrews 9:12)

"Thank God for the Blood of Jesus," for it has accomplished so much for all of humankind. Some of these accomplishments are listed below.

1. **The Blood of Jesus** – has provided a way for humankind to once again have a right relationship with God. The Word of God proclaims, "In whom we have redemption through His blood, the forgiveness of sins, according to the riches of His grace." (Ephesians 1:7)
2. **The Blood of Jesus** – has made it possible that we can begin anew, according to 2 Corinthians 5:17, which states, "Therefore if any man be in Christ, he is a new creature: old things are passed away; behold, all things are become new."
3. **The Blood of Jesus** – has washed us from our sins. Revelation 1:5-6 states, "Unto Him that loved us, and washed us from our sins in His own blood, And hath made us kings and priests unto God and His Father; to Him be glory and dominion for ever and ever. Amen."
4. **The Blood of Jesus** – has justified believers. "Much more then, being now justified by His blood, we shall be saved from wrath through Him." (Romans 5:9)
5. **The Blood of Jesus** – has given believers direct access to God, the Father. "Jesus, when He had cried again with a loud voice, yielded up the ghost. And, behold, the veil of the temple was rent in twain from the top to the bottom...." (Matthew 27:50-51)
6. **The Blood of Jesus** – has taken the sting out of death and the victory from the grave. "O death, where is thy sting? O grave, where is thy victory? And deliver them who through fear of death were all their lifetime subject to bondage." (I Corinthians 15:55; Hebrews 2:15)
7. **The Blood of Jesus** – has given us favor with God. "But God, who is rich in mercy, for His great love wherewith He loved us, Even when we were dead in sins, hath quickened us together with Christ, and hath raised us up together in heavenly places in Christ Jesus:" (Ephesians 2:4-6)

CONCLUSION

Therefore, it is clear that the blood of Jesus lifted us up out of sin and degradation; that it has cleansed us from sin; and that the shed blood of Jesus gave us the privilege to become children of the Most High God. "Now therefore ye (we) are no more strangers and foreigners, but fellow-citizens with the saints, and of the household of God." (Ephesians 2:19) **"Thank God for the Blood of Jesus."**

"A Profitable Return on Your Investment"

<u>Text</u>: <u>Mark 8:36</u> – "For what shall it profit a man, if he shall gain the whole world, and lose his own soul?"

INTRODUCTION

What a profound question Jesus asked the people and His disciples after He called them to Himself to further expound to them what it means to truly follow Him. To follow Jesus means to "deny" our self and to "take up our cross." These suggest that we must be willing to seek to do the will of God, rather than to do our own will. Jesus also cautioned them that they could expect to personally suffer for their decision to follow Him, but He assured them that their suffering would not be in vain.

DISCUSSION

It is generally accepted that when we make an investment in finances, a new company, a new innovation, etc., we expect to receive a return greater than our initial investment. Also, it is highly unlikely that any of us would knowingly make an investment in something that we know will not bring forth a profitable return, or might cause us to lose our initial investment. These principles may be applied in our spiritual walk with God. Doing the will of God is a good investment that will bring an excellent return for those of us who have subjected our will and our ways to those of God, even in times of suffering. The apostle Paul understood these principles, and he determined that the return would be well worth his investments of time, service, commitment, and suffering. Paul boldly professed in Romans 8:18, "For I reckon that the sufferings of this present time are not worthy to be compared with the glory which shall be revealed in us."

Listed below are some good investments that will bring about profitable spiritual and temporal returns.

1. **<u>Do Things God's Way</u>** – for God's thoughts are not our thoughts, and our ways are not God's ways, according to the Lord. (Isaiah 55:8-9) "For whosoever will save his life shall lose it; but whosoever shall lose his life for my sake and the gospel's, the same shall save it." (Mark 8:35)

2. **<u>Make God the Priority of Your Life</u>** - "He that loveth father or mother more than Me is not worthy of Me: and he that loveth son or daughter more than Me is not worthy of Me." (Matthew 10:37)

3. **<u>Be a Doer of the Word</u>** – "Not every one that saith unto me, Lord, Lord, shall enter into the kingdom of heaven; but he that doeth the will of my Father which is in heaven. For we must all appear before the judgment seat of Christ; that everyone may receive the things done in his body, according to that he hath done, whether it be good or bad." (Matthew 7:21; 2 Corinthians 5:10)

4. **Sow Now, and Reap Later** – "Be not deceived; God is not mocked: for whatsoever a man soweth, that shall he also reap. For he that soweth to his flesh shall of the flesh reap corruption; but he that soweth to the Spirit shall of the Spirit reap life everlasting." (Galatians 6:7)

5. **Corruptible Treasure is not profitable** – "Lay not up for yourselves treasures upon earth, where moth and rust doth corrupt, and where thieves break through and steal. But lay up for yourselves treasures in heaven, where neither moth nor rust doth corrupt, and where thieves do not break through nor steal." (Matthew 6:19-20)

CONCLUSION

Both the type and quality of your investments will directly affect our spiritual return. Investments that are outside of God's will and His ways cannot net us a profitable spiritual return. The foundation for a profitable investment was previously laid by the prophets and apostles. Jesus was, and is, that foundation. Paul said, "...I have laid the foundation, and another buildeth thereon. But let every man take heed how he buildeth thereupon. For the wisdom of this world is foolishness with God." (I Corinthians 3:10b-c,19)

"BENEFITS OF FEARING GOD"

Text: Psalm 34:9; 145:19 – "O fear the LORD, ye His saints: for there is no want to them that fear Him. He will fulfill the desire of them that fear Him: He also will hear their cry, and will save them."

INTRODUCTION

The Book of Psalms is a collection of songs and prayers that depicts the many experiences, fears, and longings of the writers. Of the one hundred fifty psalms, King David, one of Israel's greatest kings, is credited with the authorship of seventy-three of them. The remaining seventy-seven were penned by others, such as Moses, Solomon, Asaph, the sons of Korah, Heman, and Ethan. Another fifty-one of these are said to be anonymous. Oftentimes, amazing words and thoughts pour out of us during times of testing, suffering, and bondage. Such was the case with these authors. Written between the time of Moses' leadership and Israel's captivity in Babylon, these songs of praise, worship, petitions, and confessions to God mirrored the authors' personal experiences. And today, many of these psalms mirror some of the same types of situations that we may experience. Therefore, many of us have found these psalms to be quite comforting, encouraging, and strengthening to our souls.

DISCUSSION

David, in the lead texts for this lesson, reminds us that fear of the LORD gets God's attention. The word "fear" in this context is the Hebrew word yare (yaw-ray'), which means "To revere; frighten; be made afraid." It is not the same fear as the fear of snakes, neither is it anxious concern. It means, however, that our love and respect for God, as well as our concern about His terrible wrath and anger move us to humble obeisance. Listed below are eight benefits that may be derived from reverential fear of the LORD.

1. **You will be blessed** – "...Blessed is the man that feareth the LORD, that delighteth greatly in His commandments. His seed shall be mighty upon earth: the generation of the upright shall be blessed. Wealth and riches shall be in his house: and his righteousness endureth for ever." (Psalm 112:1-3)

2. **You shall receive mercy** – "For He that is mighty hath done to me great things; and holy is His name. And His mercy is on them that fear Him from generation to generation."(Luke 1:49-50)

3. **Angelic protection** – "The angel of the LORD encampeth round about them that fear Him, and delivereth them. And when they were departed, behold, the angel of the Lord appeareth to Joseph in a dream, saying, Arise, and take the young child and his mother, and flee into Egypt, and be thou there until I bring thee word; For Herod will seek the young child to destroy Him." (Psalm 34:7; Matthew 2:13)

4. **Riches, and honour, and life** – "By humility and the fear of the Lord are riches, and honour, and life." (Proverbs 22:4)

5. **Protection from calamity** – The word "calamity" refers to "an event which causes great harm, loss, disaster, or affliction." However, we are encouraged to know that "Happy is the man that feareth alway: but he that hardeneth his heart shall fall into mischief. Let not thine heart envy sinners: but be thou in the fear of the LORD all the day long." (Proverbs 28:14, 23:17)

6. **Acceptance as part of God's jewels** – "Then they that feared the LORD spake often one to another: and the LORD hearkened, and heard it, and a book of remembrance was written before Him for them that feared the LORD, and that thought upon His name. And they shall be mine, saith the LORD of hosts, in that day when I make up my jewels; and I will spare them, as a man spareth his own son that serveth him." (Malachi 3:16-17)

7. **Happiness** – "Blessed is every one that feareth the LORD; that walketh in His ways. For thou shalt eat the labour of thine hands: happy shalt thou be, and it shall be well with thee. (Psalm 128:1-2)

8. **Long life** – "The fear of the LORD prolongeth days: but the years of the wicked shall be shortened. The hope of the righteous shall be gladness: but the expectation of the wicked shall perish." (Proverbs 10:27)

CONCLUSION

And so, it is clearly evident in the Word of God that there are substantial benefits to fearing God. Our honor and reverence toward God should be our automatic responses to our God, who greatly loves and cares for us.

"STAND STILL AND SEE"

Text: Exodus 14:13, 30 – "And Moses said unto the people, Fear ye not, stand still, and see the salvation of the Lord, which He will shew to you to day: for the Egyptians whom ye have seen to day, ye shall see them again no more for ever. Thus the Lord saved Israel that day out of the hand of the Egyptians; and Israel saw the Egyptians dead upon the sea shore."

INTRODUCTION

There are times when troubles and tests arise right alongside blessings. These oftentimes cause us to fear, to be anxious, and to question God's actions and motives. The Lord God orchestrated the release from Egypt of the children of Israel. As Moses and the people fled, Pharaoh's heart was once again turned against Israel, and he was sorry that he had agreed to free them. He gathered together his people, made ready his many chariots, and pursued Israel. Israel was blessed to be free from bondage, but at the same time, Pharaoh's hot pursuit after them caused them to fear and to regret that Moses had brought them out of Egypt. They chided Moses, according to Exodus 14:12, "For it had been better for us to serve the Egyptians, than that we should die in the wilderness."

DISCUSSION

In the scriptural text for this lesson, Moses and the people are finally on their way out of Egypt. They were headed to the land that God had promised. However, Pharaoh and his armies were in hot pursuit behind them, with The Red Sea before them. The people were fearful. They blamed Moses for the position in which they found themselves. Many even regretted that they had left Egypt. It was a blessing that God delivered Israel from bondage and oppression in Egypt, but the blessing also brought about a direct threat to the newly freed people. Pharaoh and his great chariots and "Captains over every one of them" (Exodus 14:7) pursued them. Israel was very afraid, "And the children of Israel cried out unto the Lord." (Exodus 14:10) Moses told the people "Fear ye not, stand still, and see the salvation of the Lord, which He will shew to you to day: for the Egyptians whom ye have seen to day, ye shall see them again no more for ever." That which was a great blessing for Israel was later viewed by Israel as a great curse, because of the threat of immanent death that was set before them. Moses comforted the people by telling them to be not afraid, neither be anxious to take matters into their own hands. "The Lord shall fight for you, and ye shall hold your peace." (Exodus 14:14)

The message of this lesson is the same for us today, as we experience situations that come to tempt, discourage, make us afraid, cause us to doubt God, and take matters into our own hands. Let us, rather, consciously decide to do the following in the midst of challenges and adversities.

1. **"Fear not."** – We must remember that our God is omnipotent, which means that He is all-powerful. There is none more powerful than He. And, when we are in God's will,

God will fight for us. We should not despair; God is with us. No one shall be able to overtake us, for God is our help. "Stand Still and See" how God comes through for you right on time!

2. **Don't take matters into your own hands.** "Stand Still" means to allow God to direct what you do, how you do it, when you do it, and to whom you do it in times of conflict. Move only when God says for you to move. Remember, God says, "For my thoughts are not your thoughts, neither are your ways my ways...For as the heavens are higher than the earth, so are my ways higher than your ways, and my thoughts than your thoughts." (Isaiah 55:8-9)

3. **By faith, visualize the thing that you need God to do.** Israel needed God to protect them from the Egyptians and to get them over to the other side of the Red Sea. These were impossible tasks for Israel, but they were not impossible for God. Have confidence in your God. David saw Goliath's height and size, but He had confidence in his God. David said of God, "...He will deliver me out of the hand of this Philistine." God did, indeed, give David the victory. (I Samuel 17:37b)

4. **Step out on faith and move.** As Israel began to move towards the Red Sea, without knowing how they could ever cross it, God parted the sea. Israel crossed over to the other side on dry land. "And the children of Israel went into the midst of the sea upon the dry ground: and the waters were a wall unto them on their right hand, and on their left." (Exodus 14:22) Move forward by faith, as God directs, and see God work out your situation. To "Stand Still" is not passive. It is refraining from doing your own will.

5. **Know that God will be a very present help to you.** Moses told the people that "The Lord shall fight for you, and ye shall hold your peace. The children of Israel walked upon dry land in the midst of the sea; and the waters were a wall unto them on their right hand, and on their left." (Exodus 14:14, 29) God brought Israel through their crisis, God will bring you through.

6. **God will do a great work on your behalf**. "And Israel saw that great work which the Lord did upon the Egyptians: and the people feared the Lord, and believed the Lord, and His servant Moses." (Exodus 14:31)

CONCLUSION

God made a way out of no way for Israel. He will do the same for you, "For there is no respect of persons with God." (Romans 2:11) And so, when things seem so impossible, or when your world seems to be falling apart, do not yield to stress, do not give up, neither be discouraged, but **"Stand Still and See"** by faith that God is working in the midst.

"DO NOT BE A TARGET FOR THE ENEMY?"

<u>Text</u>: <u>I Peter 5:8</u> – "Be sober, be vigilant; because your adversary the devil, as a roaring lion, walketh about, seeking whom he may devour:"

INTRODUCTION

It is a known fact that Satan, the enemy of the children of God, is constantly trying to get God's people to stray away from God. Satan plants disobedient, evil, and wicked thoughts in our hearts and minds that try to distract us and to cause us to displease our God. I Peter 5:8 tells us that the adversary (our enemy) is constantly on the prowl seeking those who are weak, unprepared, and self-righteous that he might overtake them.

The Apostle Peter in his first epistle (letter) wrote to believers who, because of persecution, were "scattered throughout Pontus, Galatia, Cappadocia, Asia, and Bithynia." (I Peter 1:1). He reminded them that they were God's elect, that God loved them, and that He had neither forgotten them, nor forsaken them. He encouraged them to put more value on doing the will of God for in so doing, they would have power to say "no" to the enemy. Finally, Paul, in his epistle "to the saints which [were] at Ephesus and to the faithful in Christ Jesus," cautioned that they should not give room to the devil. They rather should put on the whole armour of God. See Ephesians 6:10-20.

The lead texts for this lesson identify some of the enemy's tactics. Not only do they tell us some of his tactics, they tell us what we can do to withstand them. Let us examine ourselves, according to I Peter 5:8 to determine if any one of us is a target for the enemy.

1. **Be sober** – "Be sober, be vigilant; because your adversary the devil, as a roaring lion, walketh about, seeking whom he may devour:" (I Peter 5:8). The word vigilant is the Greek word, nepho (nay'-fo), which means "circumspect (e.g., wary and careful about taking risks; be on guard; alert); to abstain from being drunk with wine; be discreet; watch," according to Strong's Exhaustive Concordance.

2. **Be vigilant** – gregoreuo (gray-gor-yoo'-o). This means to "keep awake; i.e., watch (literal or figurative)." You can never assume that you know all of the enemy's tactics, and that you are able to detect them whenever he decides to use them against you.

3. **Stedfastly resist the devil** – "Submit yourselves therefore to God. Resist the devil, and he will flee from you." (James 4:7) The word "resist" in the Greek is anthistemi (anth-is-tay-mee), and it means "stand against; oppose; withstand." The word "stedfast" in the Greek is stereos (ster-eh-os'), and it means "stiff, solid, strong, sure." Therefore, to "stedfastly resist" simply means to reject, without any compromise, the enemy's leading, or points-of-view about every situation he brings to us.

4. **Submit yourself to God** – The Greek word here for "submit" is hupotasso (hoop-ot-as'-so). It means for each of us to make up our mind to always endeavor to do the will of God, without regard for the situation and circumstance and with God's help. It

means to be under obedience to God, to do His will, and to emulate His ways in your life living.

5. **Hold Fast Your Godly Integrity** – "And the LORD said unto Satan, Hast thou considered my servant Job, that there is none like him in the earth, a perfect and an upright man, one that feareth God, and escheweth evil? And still he holdeth fast his integrity, although thou movedst me against him, to destroy him without cause." (Job 2:3)

6. **Don't give place to the devil** – "Beloved, believe not every spirit, but try the spirits whether they are of God: because many false prophets are gone out into the world. Be ye angry, and sin not: let not the sun go down upon your wrath: neither give place to the devil." (I John 4:1; Ephesians 4:26)

CONCLUSION

The lesson today warns us against complacency and living life with our spiritual guard down. It reminds us that our adversary, the devil, is ALWAYS on his job. His job is to devour, which is to "to drink down, i.e., gulp entire, drown, swallow up," according to Strong's Exhaustive Concordance of the Bible. So, let us not make our lives targets for Satan's attacks. Let us rather project lives that are prepared for battle, fully equipped with the whole armour of God, and confident that the battle is already won.

"A PICTURE OF A BALANCED LIFE IN CHRIST JESUS"

Text: **Matthew 22:37; Ecclesiastes 3:1** – "Jesus said unto him, Thou shalt love the Lord thy God with all thy heart, and with all thy soul, and with all thy mind. To every thing there is a season, and a time to every purpose under the heaven:"

INTRODUCTION

The Holy Scriptures are the most reliable source of information regarding that which is healthy and wholesome. Jesus's obedience to the will of His Father, and the lifestyle that He lived while He was in the earth are examples to us of a balanced life. He was not so heavenly-minded that He was no earthly good. However, the religious sect of the Pharisees was bent on keeping the letter of the Law, and neglected the heart of the laws they were charged to keep. They were perfect examples of unbalanced lives.

DISCUSSION

Jesus is the personification of a picture of the balanced life for believers. When we look at His life, we see a man who was both fully human and fully divine. However, we should be slow to use His divinity as an excuse to live less than the virtuous life that He lived, because "Forasmuch then as the children are partakers of flesh and blood, He also himself likewise took part of the same; that through death he might destroy him that had the power of death, that is, the devil." (Hebrews 2:14) Jesus balanced His physical and spiritual needs on a daily basis. He spent many hours in fervent prayer to the Father, but He did not neglect to eat. He was moved with compassion towards the sick, the poor, and those who were without the gospel. And, He did always the will of the Father.

All of the following must be done on a daily basis, with the understanding that our neglect of any one of these will cause imbalance in our life. Rather, our practice of all of these together will show how each is directly dependent upon the other, and how each is a natural progression of the other. For example, what would it profit us to be faithfully engaged in feeding the poor, and unfaithful in living a virtuous life, or in living a Word-centered life? Also, if we are faithful in reading and studying the Word of God, our application of that Word will lead us to feed the poor and to live a virtuous life. The two practiced together will help to bring balance.

Let us look at some things that can promote "A Picture of a Balanced Life in Christ Jesus."

1. **Reverence God** – Make a right relationship with God a priority in your life. "Thou shalt love the Lord thy God with all thy heart, and with all thy soul, and with all thy mind." (Matthew 22:37)

2. **Study the Word of God to know what God requires** - "Study to shew thyself approved unto God, a workman that needeth not to be ashamed, rightly dividing the word of truth." (2 Timothy 2:15)

3. **Daily live the Word of God** – Your actions will let others and God know whether you are truly a Child of God. Jesus said unto the scribes and Pharisees, "Ye hypocrites, well did Esaias prophesy of you, saying, This people draweth nigh unto Me with their mouth, and honoureth Me with their lips; but their heart is far from Me. Not every one that saith unto Me, Lord, Lord, shall enter into the kingdom of heaven; but he that doeth the will of My Father which is in heaven." (Matthew 15:8; 7:21)

4. **A life filled with compassion** – We must exemplify and practice compassion for others. "But whoso hath this world's good, and seeth his brother have need, and shutteth up his bowels of compassion from him, how dwelleth the love of God in him? When Jesus saw the multitudes, He was moved with compassion on them, because they fainted, and were scattered abroad, as sheep having no shepherd. Thou shalt love thy neighbor as thyself." (I John 3:17; Matthew 9:36, 22:39)

5. **Physical Balance** – God's desire that we take time to rejuvenate our body and our mind was factored in at Creation. "Six days shalt thou labour, and do all thy work:..." (Exodus 20:9) Also, Jesus said, "The Sabbath was made for man, and not man for the Sabbath:" (Mark 2:27). "There is nothing better for a man, than that he should eat and drink, and that he should make his soul enjoy good in his labour. This also I saw, that it was from the hand of God." (Ecclesiastes 2:24) Jesus showed physical concern for his disciples when He said, "Come ye yourselves apart into a desert place, and rest a while:" for there were many coming and going, and they had no leisure so much as to eat." (Mark 6:31)

6. **Psychological Balance** – refers to a balance between one's mind, one's will, and one's emotions. "Be careful for nothing; but in every thing by prayer and supplication with thanksgiving let your requests be made known unto God. And the peace of God, which passeth all understanding, shall keep your hearts and minds through Christ Jesus." (Philippians 4:6-7)

7. **Social Balance** – a balance between family and friends (spouse, children, church, and co-workers); believers and unbelievers. Daily develop and encourage loving relationships with others. "A man that hath friends must shew himself friendly: and there is a friend that sticketh c loser than a brother." (Proverbs 18:24)

8. **Spiritual Balance**– sets God as priority in the believer's heart and life, according to Matthew 6:33, which states, "Seek ye first the Kingdom of God and His righteousness, and all of these things shall be added unto thee." Love nothing, nor anyone, more than you love God. (Exodus 20:1-26)

CONCLUSION

In conclusion, "A Picture of A Balanced Life in Christ Jesus" is accomplished by a lifestyle that encompasses a combination of all of the above qualities. It is directly influenced by the choices that we make. Let us take a moment to examine ourselves to determine how our life might be out of balance. Then, determine the step, or steps that we need to take to achieve "A Picture of a Balanced Life in Christ Jesus."

"CURVE BALLS OF LIFE ARE NOT STRIKE OUTS"

Text: John 16:32-33 – "Behold, the hour cometh, yea, is now come, that ye shall be scattered, every man to his own, and shall leave me alone: and yet I am not alone, because the Father is with me. These things I have spoken unto you, that in me ye might have peace. In the world ye shall have tribulation: but be of good cheer I have overcome the world."

INTRODUCTION

Jesus lets us know in the Word of God that "In the world ye shall have tribulation…." (John 16:33) The word "tribulation" is the Greek word, thlipsis (thlip'sis), which means, according to Strongs Exhaustive Concordance of the Bible, "pressure (literal or figurative.); afflicted (-tion), anguish, burdened, persecution, tribulation, trouble." Therefore, we should not be surprised when any of these come upon us. We should, rather, expect to suffer in this life; we should expect to be challenged to do good, rather than evil; and we should expect to have our faith in God tested. I call these the curve balls of life.

DISCUSSION

A curve ball is a tricky pitch in baseball that has what is called a forward spin. As it approaches the batter, the ball takes a downward dive to cause the batter to miss hitting the ball. This is symbolic of some of life's situations. Oftentimes, things seem to be going well. Then all of a sudden, and without notice, negative things start to happen. These are styled as curve balls of life, which are sent to discourage us, to cause us to be stressed, and/or to cause us to fail in the matter at hand. We need to remember that a curve ball can be hit, and tribulations can be overcome. They do not necessarily have to result in strikeouts. Remember, "…in all these we are more than conquerors through Him that loved us." (Romans 8:37)

In baseball there are a variety of curve balls. Likewise, there are a variety of curve balls in life. Some of these are noted below.

1. **Curve ball of impatience** – "Thou therefore endure hardness, as a good soldier of Jesus Christ. For when God made promise to Abraham, because He could swear by no greater, He sware by Himself, saying, Surely blessing I will bless thee, and multiplying I will multiply thee. And so, after he had patiently endured, he obtained the promise." (2 Timothy 2:3; Hebrews 6:13-15.)

2. **Curve ball of deception** – Why do the wicked prosper and seem to be doing so well, while those who are living all that they know to live often struggle? God is not a respecter of persons. Jesus' death on the cross was for sinners, not for the saved. Therefore, He has patience not only with those of us who are saved and growing towards perfection, He also has patience towards those who hurt us and towards those who have not yet made a choice for Him. "The Lord is not slack concerning His promise, as some men count slackness; but is longsuffering to us-ward, not willing that any should perish, but that all should come to repentance." (2 Peter 3:9)

3. **Curve balls of trials and tribulations** – Faith must be tested. "Blessed is the man that endureth temptation: for when he is tried, he shall receive the crown of life, which the Lord hath promised to them that love Him. Wherefore lay apart all filthiness and superfluity of naughtiness, and receive with meekness the engrafted word, which is able to save your souls." (James 1:12, 21).

4. **Curve ball of worry** – "Fear thou not; for I am with thee: be not dismayed; for I am thy God: I will strengthen thee; yea, I will help thee; yea, I will uphold thee with the right hand of my righteousness. Behold, all they that are incensed against thee shall be ashamed and confounded: they shall be a nothing; and they that strive with thee shall perish." (Isaiah 41:10-11)

5. **Curve balls of hurt, disappointment, and pain** – "And God shall wipe away all tears from their eyes; and there shall be no more death, neither sorrow, nor crying, neither shall there be any more pain: for the former things are passed away." (Revelation 21:4)

6. **Curve balls of anger and discouragement** – In the midst of your pain, sorrow, disappointment, discouragement, and anger, etc., choose to worship, rather than to surrender to these negative feelings. "He that is slow to anger is better than the mighty; and he that ruleth his spirit than he that taketh a city." (Proverbs 16:32)

CONCLUSION

In conclusion, let us take our eyes off the curve balls of our life, and focus on the batter who never strikes out. Take our eyes off of our difficulties and look to God in Whom we have the victory over every curve ball of life. Finally, let our quality of life be directly influenced by our faith in God, not by the events in our life.

"PRAY: GOD ALWAYS ANSWERS PRAYER"

Texts: I John 5:14-15; Matthew 7:7 – "And this is the confidence that we have in him, that, if we ask anything according to his will, he heareth us: and if we know that he hear us, whatsoever we ask, we know that we have the petitions that we desired of him….Ask, and it shall be given you; seek, and ye shall find; knock, and it shall be opened unto you:"

INTRODUCTION

Prayer is communicating with God. It may be performed in different ways, but it must be with seriousness and humility. Through prayer, one is able to make requests, to praise God for His goodness, grace, and mercy; to worship God through adoration; to give Him thanks for His many blessings, gifts, help, daily needs, and good health; to confess one's sins, and to seek forgiveness, as we quietly listen for God's response.

DISCUSSION

One thing we must remember when we pray, and that is that we are not the only ones praying. Our requests indirectly affect the lives of others. Therefore, the LORD God in His infinite wisdom, and in His consideration of ALL of the ramifications (consequences) of the prayers offered up by His people everywhere, determines how He will answer our requests, when He will answer them, and to what extent He will answer them. We can imagine some of the conflicts in the prayer requests that ascend up to the Lord. For example, you may be praying for rain for your garden, while someone else might be praying that God holds back the rain, because he, or she is homeless and sleeps outside on the streets. God considers both requests, and then He responds to both of them, as He sees fit. A "yes" for one request will indirectly affect the life, condition, and/or circumstance of others. For example, Jesus prayed that the Father would take the cup of death away from Him. Consider what would have happened if God did what Jesus requested.

God answers prayer in a variety of ways. Some of these ways are listed below.

7. **God answers, "Yes."** - This means that we get the petition that we desired of God. Be careful to add the phrase, "if it be Your will," to protect yourself from requests that may not be in our best interest. Sometimes, God, because of our persistence in making a specific request, will grant our petition. He does so, because of His faithfulness towards us, even when God knows that it may not be in our best interest. However, He will not allow the bad choice to overtake us, but He will use the mistake as a teaching moment to show us that His will is always best.

8. **God answers, "Yes," but with changes.** - In this instance, we receive a response, but what we receive is not exactly what we requested. God knows what is best for us. Therefore, sometimes He makes a substitution that is much better than that which we originally requested. Other times, God may answer in a way that is different from the way we expected Him to respond. I am reminded of a story about a man whose house flooded after a nearby river overflowed during a historic rainstorm. He climbed on top

of his roof and prayed, "Lord, save me. Please do not let me drown." A man came by in a motorboat. He invited the man on the roof to get into the boat. The man on the roof declined. Another man came by in a row boat. He, too, invited the man on the roof to jump into the boat. Again, the man on the roof declined the invitation. Finally, one in a helicopter dropped a life line to the man on the roof. The man refused, and he drowned. When he got to heaven, he asked God, why didn't you answer my prayer? Needless to say, God answered his prayer, but not in the way the man expected. Three times the Lord God sent the man rescurers.

9. **God answers, "No,"** because the request is outside of His will; or the request is not best for us; or because the reason you want it is wrong. God is omniscient, and He can now see that which shall come to pass in the future. And, when He makes a decision, He takes the present and future into consideration. Our knowledge and understanding of issues and individuals are limited, and these are in part. I have found that it is best to let God choose what is best for us, and to accept when He says, "No." Someone told me a story about a woman who prayed for God to give her a particular man as her mate. God did not grant her request. When she saw the man years later, she was very happy that God did not grant her request. Remember, we might not understand why God denies our petition, but we shall know in retrospect.

10. **God answers, "No,"** because God decides to give us victory through the situation, rather than to remove the situation. God told Paul, "My grace is sufficient for thee: for my strength is made perfect in weakness." (2 Corinthians 12:9) God did not prevent the three Hebrew boys from being thrown into the fiery furnace, but He was in the fire with them. (Daniel 3:25) And, He brought them out. He did not prevent Daniel from being put in the lion's den. But, He shut the mouth of the lion. (Daniel 6:22)

11. **God answers, "No,"** because you can do this yourself (e.g., don't pray God prevent you from eating the chocolate cake you are about to eat, so that you will not gain additional weight.)

12. **God says, "Wait,"** because you are not ready to receive your request. Our growth is more important to God than our pleasure.

13. **God says, "Wait,"** as He prepares you for a "Yes."

CONCLUSION

Let us remember that when we pray, our prayer indirectly affects the lives of many others. God knows how best to respond, and He knows what is best for all. God is not our butler, at our beck and call to give us whatever we ask. He is rather, our Sovereign Creator, with a very broad view of His creation and our needs. "Pray: God Always Answers Prayer."

"HAVE YOU RECEIVED THE HOLY GHOST SINCE YOU BELIEVED?"

Text: **John 3:5; Acts 19:1-2** – "Verily, verily, I say unto thee, except a man be born of the water and of the Spirit, he cannot enter into the kingdom of God. And it came to pass, that, while Apollos was at Corinth, Paul having passed through the upper coasts came to Ephesus: and finding certain disciples, He said unto them, have ye received the Holy Ghost since ye believed? And they said unto him, we have not so much as heard whether there be any Holy Ghost."

INTRODUCTION

In Genesis, the first book of the Holy Scriptures, we see God, the Holy Spirit, in the beginning with God, the Father, and the Word of God. (Genesis 1:1-2). The Holy Spirit is the power of God, Whose special and/or unique earthly ministry officially began with the ascension of Jesus back to His Father, after He had accomplished God's plan of redemption for all of humankind. Jesus told His disciples, "It is expedient for you that I go away: for if I go not away, the Comforter, [which is another name for the Holy Ghost] will not come unto you; but if I depart, I will send Him unto you." (John 16:7)

DISCUSSION

The lead text reflects the response of Jesus to a question asked by a Pharisee and ruler of the Jews. Nicodemus wanted to know how a person who is old could be born again. It is important to remember that spiritual truths can only be fully understood by the Holy Spirit of God. Jesus was speaking regarding a spiritual rebirth, not a natural rebirth. This new concept was a mystery of the Kingdom of God, which Jesus introduced to the world. Natural birth is synonymous with being born of water. To be "born again" is synonymous with being born of the Holy Spirit. And, Jesus explained that these are distinct and not transferable, because "That which is born of the flesh is flesh; and that which is born of the Spirit is spirit." (John 3:6)

God's plan for humankind was greatly altered by the disobedience of one man. The need to be born again is directly attributed to this act of disobedience, for it made sinners of all of humankind. The birth, death, burial, and bodily resurrection of Jesus, the only begotten Son of God, made it possible for us to have a renewed relationship with God. After Jesus finished His work on behalf of humankind, He told His disciples "...It is expedient for you that I go away: for if I go not away, the Comforter will not come unto you; but if I depart, I will send Him unto you." (John 16:7) And, on the Day of Pentecost, the Holy Ghost descended for His ministry on the earth. "And suddenly there came a sound from heaven as of a rushing mighty wind, and it filled all the house where they were sitting. And there appeared unto them cloven tongues like as of fire, and it sat upon each of them. And they were all filled with the Holy Ghost, and began to speak with other tongues, as the Spirit gave them utterance." (Acts 2:2-4)

John's baptism was unto repentance. Spiritual rebirth is a new life in Christ Jesus through the indwelling of the Holy Spirit, Who baptizes us into Christ (I Corinthians 12:13). The Church baptizes with water, but Jesus baptizes with the Holy Ghost.

"Have You Received the Holy Ghost Since You Believed?" Come. Let us reason together and consider the following thoughts regarding the Holy Ghost.

14. **Wait for the Promise** – Jesus told His disciples, "And I will pray the Father, and He shall give you another Comforter, that He may abide with you for ever; even the Spirit of truth; whom the world cannot receive, because it seeth Him not, neither knoweth Him: but ye know Him; for He dwelleth with you, and shall be in you. But wait for the promise of the Father, which, saith He, ye have heard of me. For John truly baptized with water; but ye shall be baptized with the Holy Ghost not many days hence." (John 14:16-17; Acts 1:4-5)

15. **Present yourself before God and listen to what He is saying** – "Now therefore are we all here present before God, to hear all things that are commanded thee of God. Then Peter opened his mouth, and said, Of a truth I perceive that God is no respecter of persons: but in every nation he that feareth Him, and worketh righteousness, is accepted with Him. While Peter yet spake these words, the Holy Ghost fell on all them which heard the word. For they heard them speak with tongues, and magnify God." (Acts 10:33, 44, 46)

16. **Believers in Samaria received the Holy Ghost** – "Now when the apostles which were at Jerusalem heard that Samaria had received the word of God, they sent unto them Peter and John, who when they were come down, prayed for them, that they might receive the Holy Ghost: (for as yet He was fallen upon none of them: only they were baptized in the name of the Lord Jesus.) Then laid they their hands on them, and they received the Holy Ghost." (Acts 8:14-17)

17. **Believers in Ephesus received the Holy Ghost** – "Then said Paul, John verily baptized with the baptism of repentance, saying unto the people, that they should believe on Him which should come after Him, that is, on Christ Jesus. When they heard this, they were baptized in the name of the Lord Jesus. And when Paul had laid his hands upon them, the Holy Ghost came on them; and they spake with tongues, and prophesied." (Acts 19:4-6)

CONCLUSION

God knew that we would need power in order to live the life He has ordained for us. This life can only be lived through the Spirit of God's power and His leading. The ministry of the Holy Spirit is a continuation of God's plan of salvation, as well as His plan to preserve us on the earth until the second coming of our Lord Jesus, the Christ. **"HAVE YOU RECEIVED THE HOLY GHOST SINCE YOU BELIEVED?"**

"MADE IN GOD'S IMAGE AND LIKENESS"

Text: **Genesis 1:26-28; 2:7** - "And God said, Let us make man in our image, after our likeness: and let them have dominion over the fish of the sea, and over the fowl of the air, and over the cattle, and over all the earth, and over every creeping thing that creepeth upon the earth. So God created man in His own image, in the image of God created He him; male and female created He them."

INTRODUCTION

When we think of the image of a thing, we generally mean that one thing resembles another. The Hebrew word for the word "image" is tselem (tseh'-lem), which is from "a root which means, to shade," according to Strong's Exhaustive Concordance. Figuratively, it means, "illusion, resemblance; hence a representative figure," the book explains. The word, "likeness" is the Hebrew word demuwth (dem-ooth'), and it has a similar meaning, which means "resemblance; model; shape; like; manner; or similitude." For example, a glove is shaped like a hand, and it resembles the characteristics of a hand in that it has five finger-shaped spaces for the fingers to be inserted. Two of these spaces are shorter in length just as two of the fingers of the hand. The glove is the image and likeness of the hand.

DISCUSSION

The image and likeness of God means that man was made and given to possess the same spiritual likeness and characteristics of God, his Creator. I say spiritual characteristics, because God is Spirit. And, when He said "Let us make man in our image, after our likeness," He was speaking to the Word and to the Holy Spirit of God, Who are also Spirit. He made man pure and holy to live eternally on the earth in that state. God made man to reproduce other seed that would be holy and to populate the earth. God gave him a body, which was different from Himself, and He breathed the breath of life into man's nostrils, and man became a living soul for the work that he would perform on the earth. This provided man the ability to communicate with other people, to discover, achieve, and to make physical progress in the world that he was to populate.

Christ Jesus was our perfect example of the image and likeness of God in regard to His character and attributes. And, though He was both fully human and fully divine, we are to reflect His image and likeness in our bodies and in our living. We were predestined by God to be conformed to the image of His Son, as noted in Romans 8:29. And, as new creatures in Christ Jesus, let us "Put on the new man, which after God is created in righteousness and true holiness." (Ephesians 4:24) Listed below are some ways we can exemplify and walk in the image and likeness of God, as Jesus did in this present world.

1. **Seek to do always the will of God** – Jesus said, "For I came down from heaven, not to do mine own will, but the will of Him that sent me...and to finish His work." (John 6:38, 4:34)

2. **Allow God to use you for His purposes** – The main purpose for the coming of Jesus was to make a way for unholy humankind to once again have personal relationship with the Holy God; to destroy the works of the devil. For the Son of man is some to seek and to save that which was lost. And ye know that He was manifested to take away our sins; and in Him is no sin. Wherefore in all things it behoved Him to be made like unto His brethren, that He might be a merciful and faithful high priest in things pertaining to God, to make reconciliation for the sins of the people. We, too, are to be God's agents to lead men, women, and children out of sin and degradation and to restoration with God, their Creator. Go ye into all the world, and preach the gospel to every creature. He that believeth and is baptized shall be saved; but he that believeth not shall be damned. (I John 3:8; Luke 19:10; I John 3:5; Hebrews 2:17; Mark 16:15-16)

3. **Become one with God** - To become one with God simply means to deny ourselves and embrace God's will and His ways, and then apply them in our daily living. Jesus was one with the Father. He said, "I and my Father are one." (John 10:30)

4. **Be God's model in the earth** – By surrendering your body for God's use and purposes in the earth, you become a reflection of God with us. "I beseech you therefore, brethren, by the mercies of God, that ye present your bodies a living sacrifice, holy, acceptable unto God, which is your reasonable service. And be not conformed to this world: but be ye transformed by the renewing of your mind, that ye may prove what is that good, and acceptable, and perfect, will of God." (Romans 12:1-2)

5. **Possess and manifest the fruit in the earth** - To be in the image and likeness of God means to live in accord with the Word of God and the Holy Spirit of God, Who grows His fruit in us. "But the fruit of the Spirit is love, joy, peace, longsuffering, gentleness, goodness, faith, meekness, temperance: against such there is no law. And they that are Christ's have crucified the flesh with the affections and lusts." (Galatians 5:22-24)

CONCLUSION

At creation, Adam was pure, holy, and righteous in the image of the invisible God. But, his disobedience brought about stain upon his image, and it severed his personal relationship with his God. Yet, God did not cast Adam and Eve aside. God covered their nakedness, and devised a new plan for restoration of relationship with Him. Jesus is the foundation of that plan. He fully accomplished the plan of God through His death, burial, and bodily resurrection. Jesus made it possible for every one of us who believes in Him as our personal Lord and Savior to be baptized into the fullness of His Holy Spirit. Finally, through Christ Jesus we may once again be in the image and likeness of God.

"THE UNIQUENESS OF JESUS"

TEXT: **Luke 24:36-39** – "And as they thus spake, Jesus Himself stood in the midst of them, and saith unto them, Peace be unto you. But they were terrified and affrighted, and supposed that they had seen a spirit. And He said unto them, why are ye troubled? and why do thoughts arise in your hearts? Behold my hands and my feet, that it is I Myself: handle me, and see; for a spirit hath not flesh and bones, as ye see me have."

INTRODUCTION

Jesus was not an ordinary man. He was truly unique. The word, "unique," is described by Merriam-Webster's dictionary as, "Used to say that something, or someone is unlike anything, or anyone else; very special, or unusual; belonging to, or connected with only one particular thing, place, or person." What a perfect word to describe Jesus, our Lord and Savior. He is the only one whose uniqueness is that He was both fully human and fully divine

DISCUSSION

As believers, we spend much of our spiritual witness convincing non-believers of all that Jesus accomplished for them in the pardon of their sins. We tell them that according to the Holy Scriptures, Jesus was God's only begotten Son; that He was spiritually conceived by the Holy Spirit of God; and that He was born of a young girl who was a virgin. This is a portion of the evidence for our belief that He was fully God. Then, we tell them of the many works and miracles that He performed while He was in the earth. However, these were works and miracles that only God could perform, which further established that Jesus was God in the flesh. His greatest accomplishment was to become humankind's only way back to the Father. Although His spiritual accomplishment is the most significant, and it determines our eternal destiny with, or without God, we should not neglect to remember that Jesus, our Lord and Savior, was also fully human. Therefore, Jesus was both fully human and fully divine. There is no other creature that can make this claim and it be true. He was truly unique.

Some examples of "The Uniqueness of Jesus" are noted below.

1. **Jesus pre-existed in the beginning with God, and He was God** – Jesus existed in the beginning with God in the spirit world as the Word of God. "In the beginning was the Word, and the Word was with God, and the Word was God." (John 1:1)

2. **Jesus was active in the Creation of all things** – He was the Word that went forth out of the mouth of the Father and created that which was spoken. "All things were made by Him; and without Him was not any thing made that was made. But to us there is but one God, the Father, of whom are all things, and we in Him; and one Lord Jesus Christ, by whom are all things, and we by Him." (John 1:3; I Corinthians 8:6)

3. **The Word became flesh** – "Therefore the Lord Himself shall give you a sign; Behold, a virgin shall conceive, and bear a son, and shall call His name Immanuel. And the Word was made flesh, and dwelt among us, (and we beheld His glory, the glory as of the only begotten of the Father,) full of grace and truth. The Apostle Matthew wrote regarding Immanuel, "And

when they were come into the house, they saw the young child with Mary His mother, and fell down, and worshipped Him:" (Isaiah 7:14; John 1:14; Matthew 2:11)

4. **Human beings have a body – Jesus had a body** – The Word was made flesh for the work He was to accomplish on behalf of salvation. "Sacrifice and offering thou wouldest not, but a body hast thou prepared me. Then said I, Lo, I come (in the volume of the book it is written of me,) to do thy will, O God. And when they were come to the place, which is called Calvary, there they crucified Him…(Hebrews 10:5, 7; Luke 23:33;)

5. **Jesus gave His body for the sins of humankind** – "Who gave Himself for our sins, that He might deliver us from this present evil world, according to the will of God and our Father: To whom be glory for ever and ever. Amen." (Galatians 1:4-5)

6. **He rose bodily from the grave** – After His death and burial, Jesus was bodily raised by the power of the Holy Spirit of God. He told his disciples, "Behold my hands and my feet, that it is I myself: handle me, and see; for a spirit hath not flesh and bones, as ye see me have." (John 24:39)

7. **Jesus ascended back to heaven after His work was finished** – Jesus proclaimed, "And no man hath ascended up to heaven, but he that came down from heaven, even the Son of man which is in heaven…while they beheld, He was taken up; and a cloud received Him out of their sight. And while they looked stedfastly toward heaven as He went up, behold, two men stood by them in white apparel; (John 3:13; Acts 1:10)

CONCLUSION

Therefore, the "Uniqueness of Jesus" is most clearly seen in His pre-existence, His birth, His works, His death, His resurrection, and His ascension. In biblical times many suffered death by crucifixion, but the crucifixion of Jesus was also truly unique. "Now from the sixth hour there was darkness over all the land unto the ninth hour." (Matthew 27:45) It was a common practice to break the bones of the person who was crucified to

hasten his death, but Jesus' bones were not broken, because His spirit had already departed when the soldier came to break His bones (John 19:32); all that He suffered was in fulfillment of the Holy Scriptures (John 19:36-37); "…the veil of the temple was rent in twain from the top to the bottom; and the earth did quake, and the rocks rent; and the graves were opened; and many bodies of the saints which slept arose, and came out of the graves after His resurrection, and went into the holy city, and appeared unto many." (Matthew 27:51-53) Jesus made salvation possible for all who will believe in Him, "Neither is there salvation in any other: for there is none other name under heaven given among men, whereby we must be saved." (Acts 4:12) No other human being can claim like experiences and they be true. These reflect the "Uniqueness of Jesus."

The humanity of Jesus is confirmed in His physical attributes, His necessities, and His habits, which are common to all humankind. Some of these commonalities include the following: He was born of a woman; He grew up after His birth; He became tired, thirsty, and hungry; He was tempted by the adversary; He had emotions; and He had freewill. He came in the flesh that He might die for our sins and show us how to live in obedience to the will of God in this present world. Jesus is our perfect example of how to live in this present world, without being of the world.

"JESUS LOVES US"

TEXT: <u>Romans 5:6-8</u> - "For when we were yet without strength, in due time Christ died for the ungodly. For scarcely for a righteous man will one die: yet peradventure for a good man some would even dare to die. But God commendeth His love toward us, in that, while we were yet sinners, Christ died for us."

INTRODUCTION

This lesson is to proclaim that in spite of our current situation, or condition; in spite of how hopeless things may seem; in spite of the many terrible things that we may have done in our life; and in spite of our rejection of God, "Jesus Loves Us." Just as the love of our natural parents does not generally cease towards their rebellious and disobedient children, God's love for His rebellious and disobedient children also does not cease. In both instances, however, the actions of the children may temporarily separate them from an ongoing relationship with their parents; the love of the parents for their child will still desire a positive relationship with their child. So it is with God. God loves us.

DISCUSSION

Rebellion and disobedience are sins, and sin separates us from God. Therefore, GOD devised a plan of restoration that is acceptable to Him. That plan is revealed to us in John 3:15-16, which says, "For God so loved the world, that He gave His only begotten Son, that whosoever believeth in Him should not perish, but have everlasting life. For God sent not His Son into the world to condemn the world; but that the world through Him might be saved." God loves you, and so does Jesus, His Son.

Jesus is God's remedy for our restoration to fellowship with Him. It is because of what Jesus did that we may once again have relationship with God. The love of Jesus for you and for me, was exemplified in His willingness to die for us, while we were yet weak, without power to continue to do the things that are good and right, without power to resist evil, and unstable in all of our ways. "For scarcely for a righteous man will one die: yet peradventure for a good man some would even dare to die. But God commendeth His love toward us, in that, while we were yet sinners, Christ died for us." (Romans 5:7-8)

Therefore, we can know that "Jesus Loves Us," because of the following facts.

1. **He denied Himself for our sakes** – When Jesus knew that His time had come, He prayed to His Father at the Garden of Gethsemane that the cup of suffering be removed from Him. But, He ended that prayer in humble submission to the will of God, when He said, "Nevertheless not my will, but thine, be done. Again, the onlookers at His crucifixion chided Him saying, "He saved others; Himself He cannot save. If He be the King of Israel, let Him now come down from the cross, and we will believe Him." Love for us kept Jesus on the cross. (Luke 22:42; Matthew 27:42)

2. **He forgave us our transgressions against Him** – "Jesus Loves Us," because as He was being crucified, He prayed "Father, forgive them; for they know not what they do." (Luke 23:34)

3. **Jesus became a ransom for us** - "For even the Son of man came not to be ministered unto, but to minister, and to give His life a ransom for many." (Mark 10:45)

4. **He boldly displayed His love** – His love for us was boldly displayed on the cross at Calvary. "For scarcely for a righteous man will one die: yet peradventure for a good man some would even dare to die. Greater love hath no man than this, that a man lay down his life for his friends." (Romans 5:7; John 15:13)

5. **God calls us His children** - "Behold, what manner of love the Father hath bestowed upon us, that we should be called the sons of God: therefore the world knoweth us not, because it knew Him not." (I John 3:1)

6. **He has begun a good work in us** - "Being confident of this very thing, that He which hath begun a good work in you will perform it until the day of Jesus Christ:" (Philippians 1:6)

CONCLUSION

Finally, we know that "Jesus Loves Us," because of all that He has willingly suffered on our behalf. Through His life and His works, Jesus satisfied the implications of an old adage which say, "Love is not what it says; love is what it does." We believe and do know that "Greater love hath no man than this, that a man lay down his life for his friends." (John 15:13) Thank God that we are friends of Jesus.

Lesson Number Thirteen

"JESUS: THE WAY, THE TRUTH, AND THE LIFE"

Text: John 14:5-7 - "Thomas saith unto Him, Lord, we know not whither Thou goest; and how can we know the way? Jesus saith unto him, 'I am the way, the truth, and the life: no man cometh unto the Father, but by Me. If ye had known Me, ye should have known My Father also, and from henceforth ye know Him, and have seen Him."

INTRODUCTION

Like Thomas, many are asking, where is the way? Give me an address, so that I can Google it, or put it in my GPS. However, we fail to realize that this way is not a thoroughfare for travel, neither is it a course of travel from place-to-place, as is described in Merriam-Webster's Dictionary and Thesaurus. It is a person. A believer who desires to spend eternal life in heaven with God cannot get to that destination but by Him. In this lesson, we will explore just what Jesus meant, when He professed, "I am the way, the truth, and the life."

DISCUSSION

Strong's Exhaustive Concordance describes the word, "WAY," in this text as "a road; by implication a progress (the route, act or distance); figurative, a mode or means: journey, (high-)way." When the article "the" is placed in front of the word, it signifies only one specific path to a destination, and that path is Jesus. The truth of the matter further contends that Jesus is not only the way, but He is also the ticket that is needed for entrance at the destination. Jesus is the way to know God. We know of God by our study of the Word of God, through listening to the preaching and teaching of the Word. We get to truly know God through personal relationship with Christ Jesus and the baptism by the Holy Ghost. A life that is united with Jesus unites us with God the Father in character and in essence.

In this lesson, we will explore Jesus' statement, "I am the way, the truth, and the life." Let us begin our discussion with the phrase, **"Jesus is the Way."** Jesus is the Way for the following reasons:

1. **He is the only means by which we can get to the Father** – "No man cometh unto the Father, but by me." (Acts 14:6)

2. **We cannot have relationship with the Father, except through the Son** – A life that is in true relationship with Jesus is also in true relationship with God, the Father in both character and in essence. "Whosoever denieth the Son, the same hath not the Father: (but) he that acknowledgeth the Son hath the Father also." (John 10:30-31; I John 2:23)

3. **He is the only route to eternal life** – There is no secondary, or alternate way to eternal life with God. The true way is a restrictive channel, because as Jesus said, "...Strait is the gate, and narrow is the way, which leadeth unto life, and few there be that find it." (Matthew 7:14)

4. **He speaks for us before the Father** – "Whosoever therefore shall confess me before men, him will I confess also before my Father which is in heaven." (Matthew 10:32)

The word **"Truth"** in this text means "true, truly, verity, as not concealing," according to Strong's. Truth is "factual, real, and certain." In other words, Jesus is "the real deal;" the very essence of all that is right, good, and just. He is the only measuring stick by which we can determine the actuality of a matter, or a thing. **"Jesus is the Truth,"** because of the following:

1. **The truth has made us free from sin, shame, and condemnation** – Jesus said, "And ye shall know the truth, and the truth shall make you free. For God so loved the world, that He gave His only begotten Son, that whosoever believeth in Him should not perish, but have everlasting life. If the Son therefore shall make you free, ye shall be free indeed." (John 8:32, 3:16, 8:36)
2. **He spoke what the Father instructed** – "For I have not spoken of myself; but the Father which sent me, He gave me a commandment, what I should say, and what I should speak." (John 12:49)
3. **He did the will of the Father** – "For I came down from heaven, not to do mine own will, but the will of Him that sent Me." (John 6:38)
4. **The witness of the Father** – "While he yet spake, behold, a bright cloud overshadowed them: and behold a voice out of the cloud, which said, This is my beloved Son, in whom I am well pleased; hear ye Him." (Matthew 17:5)

The narrative about the death and resurrection of Lazarus, a very special friend of Jesus, highlights the fact that **"Jesus is the Life."** He is the life for those who are dead in sins and for those who are dead in the body. When Jesus arrived at Bethany, Lazarus was already dead. Nevertheless, Martha showed confidence in Jesus when she said, "Lord, if thou hadst been here, my brother had not died." (John 11:21) Jesus's replied, "Thy brother shall rise again." (John 11:23) Martha let Jesus know that she was aware that her brother would rise again at the last day. Jesus let her know that He was the personification of the resurrection, and the life. She would not need to wait until the last day, because "I am the resurrection, and the life: he that believeth in me, though he were dead, yet shall he live: And whosoever liveth and believeth in me shall never die...." (John 11:25-26) Therefore, **"Jesus is the Life,"** because of the following:

1. **They that believe have passed from death unto life** – "...He that heareth my word, and believeth on Him that sent me, hath everlasting life, and shall not come into condemnation; but is passed from death unto life." (John 5:24)
2. **The Father hath given the power of life to the Son** – "For as the Father hath life in Himself; so hath He given to the Son to have life in Himself." (John 5:26)
3. **He is the Bread of Life** – "...Moses gave you not that bread from heaven; but My Father giveth you the true bread from heaven. For the Bread of God is He which cometh down from heaven, and giveth life unto the world." (John 6:32-33)
4. **He bodily raised others from the dead** – Jesus said, "Lazarus come forth. And he that was dead came forth, bound hand and foot with grave clothes: and his face was bound about with a napkin. Jesus said unto them, Loose him, and let him go." (John 11:43-44)

CONCLUSION

And so, let us be assured that **"Jesus IS the Way, the Truth, and the Life."** In Him, we have all that we need in this life, as well as all that will be needed in the life to come. God has made His love and mercy toward us visibly known through Christ Jesus, "Who for the joy that was set before Him endured the cross, despising the shame, and is set down at the right hand of the throne of God." Thank God for Jesus!

"MORE THAN A PROPHET AND TEACHER: JESUS IS LORD"

Text: **John 4:42** - "And many more believed because of His own word; And said unto the woman, Now we believe, not because of thy saying: for we have heard Him ourselves, and know that this is indeed the Christ, the Savior of the World."

INTRODUCTION

This lesson is to show that Jesus was more than a prophet and a teacher. To many He was a prophet, because He was able to unveil matters that were previously unknown and to foretell events before they occurred. This ability, however, was the result of Jesus' being fully human and fully divine at the same time. The lesson text specifically refers to the encounter of a Samaritan woman with Jesus. Jesus was able to tell her about all of her personal sins, and to offer her the Living Water of redemption. She was astonished and convinced that Jesus was a prophet. She went into the city to tell others about Jesus, and to invite them to come see Him and to hear Him.

DISCUSSION

Jesus confounded all with whom He came in contact, as He ministered on earth. Multitudes of people came to listen to His teachings and to be healed of their sicknesses and infirmities. "He taught as one having authority, and not as the scribes," according to Matthew 7:29. Jesus taught in the synagogue, in the temple, and throughout the regions of the country. His message was one of salvation. The Holy Scriptures state, "For the Son of man is come to seek and to save that which was lost." (Luke 19:10) Some of the people called Him a prophet, and some acknowledged Him as being a good teacher. But, Jesus was more than both of these. He was, and is, Lord. The Word of God says the following about Jesus:

1. **Jesus is the image of the invisible God** – "...Who hath delivered us from the power of darkness, and hath translated us into the kingdom of His dear Son: in Whom we have redemption through His blood, even the forgiveness of sins: who is the image of the invisible God, the firstborn of every creature." (Colossians 1:13-15)

2. **Jesus is Lord and Master** – "Ye call me Master and Lord: and ye say well; for so I am." (John 13:13)

3. **Jesus reigns in the heavens and on the earth** – "All power is given unto me in heaven and in earth." (Matthew 28:18)

4. **God made Him to be Lord** – "Therefore let all the house of Israel know assuredly, that God hath made that same Jesus, whom ye crucified, both Lord and Christ," (Acts 2:36)

5. **Jesus reigns over all principalities and powers** – "And what is the exceeding greatness of His power to us-ward who believe, according to the working of His mighty power, Which He wrought in Christ, when He raised Him from the dead, and

set Him at his own right hand and in the heavenly places, Far above all principality, and power, and might, and dominion, and every name that is named, not only in this world, but also in that which is to come: And hath put all things under His feet, and gave Him to be the head over all things to the church, Which is His body, the fulness of Him that filleth all in all." (Ephesians 1:19-23)

6. **The heavenly hosts shall acknowledge Him** – "And the seventh angel sounded; and there were great voices in heaven, saying, the Kingdoms of this world are become the kingdoms of our Lord, and of His Christ; and He shall reign for ever and ever." (Revelation 11:15; 19:16)

7. **Thomas called Him Lord** – "And Thomas answered and said unto him, My Lord and my God. Jesus saith unto him, Thomas, because thou hast seen me, thou hast believed; blessed are they that have not seen, and yet have believed." (John 20:28-29)

CONCLUSION

Jesus was, indeed, more than a prophet and teacher. He is Lord over all in and on the earth. Adam was the first man on the earth. Jesus is called the second Adam. Yet, according to the Holy Word of God, Jesus is the Lord from heaven. (I Corinthians 15:47) "But to us there is but one God, the Father, of whom are all things, and we in Him; and one Lord Jesus Christ, by whom are all things, and we by Him." (I Corinthians 8:6) Believe these things, and praise Him for being our Savior and Lord.

"KEEP YOUR GIFTS: JUST DO WHAT GOD SAYS"

Texts: **I Samuel 15:1-11, 22** – " It repenteth me that I have set Saul to be king: for he is turned back from following me, and hath not performed my commandments. And it grieved Samuel; and he cried unto the Lord all night. And Samuel said, Hath the Lord as great delight in burnt offerings and sacrifices, as in obeying the voice of the Lord? Behold, to obey is better than sacrifice, and to hearken than the fat of rams."

INTRODUCTION

The text for this lesson shares a conversation between Saul, Israel's first king, and the prophet Samuel. The Lord God sent Samuel with a message to Saul regarding Amalek and his people. Samuel told Saul, "Thus saith the LORD of hosts, I remember that which Amalek did to Israel, how he laid wait for him in the way, when he came up from Egypt. Now go and smite Amalek, and utterly destroy all that they have, and spare them not; but slay both man and woman, infant and suckling, ox and sheep, camel and ass." (I Samuel 15:2-3) This is a good example of one of the many ways the Lord God works. He may not give us a full explanation of all that He is doing, or why He has chosen to do things in a particular way. But, we should be careful to remember that God tells us in His Word, "For my thoughts are not your thoughts, neither are your ways my ways...." (Isaiah 55:8) Therefore, our focus should be on just doing what the Lord says for us to do.

DISCUSSION

To God, obedience to His commands is better than all of the offerings, talents, services, etc. that we may be able to offer Him. Oftentimes, God does not give us His full perspective on a situation, because He wants us to put our trust in Him and to know that what He has determined is the best decision to accomplish His will for that situation. God's plans are never without purpose. However, our obedience to God's command leads to fulfillment of God's revealed and unrevealed purposes for a situation. Disobedience short circuits God's plan and unrevealed purpose in a situation, and it brings the wrath of God upon the ones to whom the command was given. Therefore, we should know and be careful to obey whatever God says, even though, and especially when, we may not understand WHY He gave the command.

In this narrative, God told Saul that He remembered what Amalek did to Israel when God delivered Israel out of bondage in Egypt. God gave specific instructions that were to be carried out by Saul. However, God did not reveal to Saul the intent and goal of His instructions. Saul obeyed God in part. He followed his own whims and the whims of the people, who convinced him to spare, Agag, the king of the Amalekites and the best of the animals to sacrifice unto the Lord. Everything that was repulsive and worthless, Saul completely destroyed. These actions were not according to God's instructions, and God was sorry that He had made Saul to be king of Israel. The moral of this lesson is, if we want to please God, we should be careful to do exactly what God says, and exactly how God says for us to do it. If we do things differently, we turn from following God, and we do not perform God's commandments. Samuel summed up Saul's actions with a question. "Hath the Lord as great delight in burnt-offerings and sacrifices, as in obeying the voice of the Lord?" (I Samuel 15:22) Samuel did not wait for Saul's response, but replied, "Behold, to obey is better than sacrifice, and to hearken than the fat of rams." (I Samuel 15:22) In other words, "Keep Your Gifts: Just Do What God Says." God does not want, and He will not accept gifts that are the result of our disobedience. To God obedience is more important than gifts that we may offer.

Suggestions that can help us to obey God's commands include the following:

1. **Love God** – "He that hath my commandments, and keepeth them, he it is that loveth Me: and he that loveth Me shall be loved of My Father, and I will love him, and will manfest Myself to Him." (John 14:21)

2. **Allow God's will to be done through us** – "Now go and smite Amalek, and utterly destroy all that they have, and spare them not; but slay both man and woman, infant and suckling, ox and sheep, camel and ass." (I Samuel 15:3) Jesus allowed God to use Him to make salvation available to all who believe in Him. "And being made perfect, He became the author of eternal salvation unto all them that obey Him;" (Hebrews 5:9)

3. **Obey God rather than men** – "...For the people spared the best of the sheep and of the oxen, to sacrifice unto the Lord thy God; and the rest we have utterly destroyed. But the people took of the spoil, sheep and oxen, the chief of the things which should have been utterly destroyed, to sacrifice unto the Lord thy God in Gilgal." (I Samuel 15:15, 21)

4. **Accept that it is our duty to obey God** – "Let us hear the conclusion of the whole matter: Fear God, and keep His commandments: for this is the whole duty of man." (Ecclesiastes 12:13)

5. **Don't try to understand God's will and ways** – "Trust in the Lord with all thine heart; and lean not unto thine own understanding. For My thoughts are not your thoughts, neither are your ways My ways, saith the Lord. For as the heavens are higher than the earth, so are My ways higher than your ways, and My thoughts than your thoughts." (Proverbs 3:5; Isaiah 55:8-9)

6. **Remember that God requires full compliance** – "And Samuel came to Saul: and Saul said unto him, Blessed be thou of the Lord: I have performed the commandment of the Lord. And Samuel said, What meaneth then this bleating of the sheep in mine ears, and the lowing of the oxen which I hear?" (I Samuel 15:13-14)

CONCLUSION

Have you ever felt led by God to do something? Instead, you modified God's instructions by adding to it, changing it, or taking away from that which God had commanded. What were the consequences you suffered? Obedience means doing fully that which God has commanded. Therefore, we should remember that we can never improve that which God has given. **"Keep your gifts: Just Do What God Says."**

"OUR GOD IS FAITHFUL: NO NEED TO COMPROMISE"

Text: **Daniel 3:15** – "Now if ye be ready that at what time ye hear the sound of the cornet, flute, harp, sackbut, psaltery, and dulcimer, and all kinds of musick, ye fall down and worship the image which I have made; well: but if ye worship not, ye shall be cast the same hour into the midst of a burning fiery furnace; and who is that God that shall deliver you out of my hands?"

INTRODUCTION

The text for this lesson is both a pictorial and an historical account of one horrendous experience of three Hebrew boys. They were taken from Jerusalem and relocated to Babylon when King Nebuchadnezzar besieged the city. It was a standard practice of captors to change the names of those whom they captured, and to carry out deliberate plans to break down and transform their cultural and religious mores. Shadrach, Meshach, and Abednego were no exceptions to this practice, but they refused to conform. The King set up a golden image, and commanded that when the people hear the music, that they fall down and worship the image. The Hebrew boys, however, remembered the teachings of their fathers and of the Holy Scriptures, which state, "I, even I, am He that comforteth you: who art thou, that thou shouldest be afraid of a man that shall die, and of the son of man which shall be made as grass; Thou shalt have no other gods before me. Thou shalt not make unto thee any graven image, or any likeness of any thing that is in heaven above, or that is in the earth beneath, or that is in the water under the earth: Thou shalt not bow down thyself to them, nor serve them:" (Isaiah 51:12; Exodus 20:3-5a)

DISCUSSION

Daniel, one of the Major Prophets, relates this story of the experience of his three Hebrew friends. He addressed this writing to others who were captives in Babylon and to all of God's people. At this time, Daniel was also a captive in Babylon. His name, and the names of the three Hebrew boys were changed to Babylonian names in accordance with pagan practice to redirect their allegiance from the God of Israel and His teachings to the gods of Babylon. Daniel's name was changed to Belteshazzar; Hananiah's name to Shadrach; Mishael's name to Meshach; and Azariah's name to Abed-nego. Neither Daniel nor the Hebrew boys agreed to worship the idol gods of Babylon, even when they were under threat of death. They chose to stand firm on their faith in the God of Abraham, Isaac, and Jacob. They professed that their God was well able to deliver them from the "burning fiery furnace" and out of the king's hands. Even after the furnace was heated seven times hotter than normal; as they were being bound up with their clothes and hats still on them; and as they were being prepared to be thrown into the fiery furnace, not one of the boys denied their God, nor conformed to the wishes of the king. God was faithful; He was present with them in the midst of the fire, and finally, He delivered them from the effects of the fire. (See Daniel 3:27)

In this life, we will also be tested and tried. The three Hebrew boys show us how to apply our faith and trust in our God, even when we are under threat of losing our life. Consider the following.

1. **Apply the principles of your faith when you are tried** – "There are certain Jews whom thou hast set over the affairs of the province of Babylon, Shadrach, Meshach, and Abed-nego; these men, O king, have not regarded thee: they serve not thy gods, nor worship the golden image which thou hast set up." (Daniel 3:12)

2. **Stand firm in your faith even when you are confronted by leaders** – "O Nebuchadnezzar, we are not careful to answer thee in this matter. If it be so, our God whom we serve is able to deliver us from the burning fiery furnace, and He will deliver us out of thine hand, O king. But if not, be it known unto thee, O king, that we will not serve thy gods, nor worship the golden image which thou hast set up." (Daniel 3:17-18)

3. **Do not fear when things seem to be falling apart** – the furnace was heated seven times hotter; the boys were bound in their clothes, hats, and other garments that would cause a great burning. "And these three men, Shadrach, Meshach, and Abed-nego, fell down into the midst of the burning fiery furnace. Then, Nebuchadnezzar the king was astonied, and rose up in haste, and spake, and said unto his counsellors, Did not we cast three men bound into the midst of the fire? Lo, I see four men loose, walking in the midst of the fire, and they have no hurt; and the form of the fourth is like the Son of God." (Daniel 3:23-25)

4. **Be willing to accept God's way of deliverance** - God did not prevent the Hebrews from being thrown into the fiery furnace, but He met them in the midst of the fire. "...He will deliver us out of thine hand, O king." (Daniel 3:17)

CONCLUSION

God's faithfulness is revealed throughout the Holy Scriptures. We can depend on God. We must be stedfast in our trust in God, as we are confronted with various personal challenges. Let us remember that the Word of God promises us that "There hath no temptation taken you but such as is common to man: but God is faithful, who will not suffer you to be tempted above that ye are able; but will with the temptation also make a way to escape, that ye may be able to bear it." (I Corinthians 10:13)

"LOVING JESUS IS MORE THAN A PROFESSION"

<u>Text</u>: <u>Mark 12:29-31</u> - "The first of all the commandments is, Hear, O Israel; The Lord our God is one Lord: And thou shalt love the Lord thy God with all thy heart, and with all thy soul, and with all thy mind, and with all thy strength: this is the first commandment. And the second is like, namely this, thou shalt love thy neighbor as thyself. There is none other commandment greater than these."

INTRODUCTION

This lesson stresses the deep spiritual meaning of what it means to truly love God. The proof is not in the words we speak, neither is it in the works that we perform. The full manifestation of our love for God is revealed in our obedience to His will and His ways. "Loving God is More Than a Profession."

DISCUSSION

The scribes came to Jesus and asked, "Which is the first commandment of all?" Jesus replied with the words that are noted above in our Lesson Text. In His response, Jesus let them know that they must give God precedence in all things pertaining to their lives. The superlative "all" suggests that nothing, nor anyone is excepted.

The heart, soul, mind, and strength combined make up our person. According to <u>Webster's Dictionary</u>, the heart is "a muscular organ whose rhythmic contraction keeps up the circulation of the blood in the body." However, from a spiritual perspective, the heart is much more than a muscular organ; it is the seat of our inner most being, emotions, and moral fiber. Whatever is stored up in our hearts will directly affect our personal relationship with God and others. A pure heart is required of all who truly love God, for the scripture says, "Blessed are the pure in heart: for they shall see God" (Matthew 5:8).

The soul of man is the "seat" of our emotions. It expresses our moments of sorrow, joy, compassion, hurt, etc. within the heart. As Jesus waited for the soldiers to come and take Him away for His crucifixion, He told his disciples, "My soul is exceeding sorrowful, even unto death: tarry ye here, and watch with Me." (Matthew 26:38)

The mind is the "seat" of our intellect, but it is finite regarding the things of God. We can only know God through His own revelation of Himself in the Holy Scriptures. His will and His ways are outlined for us in the Bible. "O the depth of the riches both of the wisdom and knowledge of God! how unsearchable are His judgments, and His ways past finding out! For who hath known the mind of the Lord? or who hath been His counsellor?" (Romans 11:33-34) To love God with all of our mind is to subject all that we know and think to the scrutiny and acceptance of God's revealed will.

To love God with all of our strength means to love God with our whole being, which includes our heart, our soul, our mind, and strength. These are to be used to resist evil through the power of the Holy Spirit for the glory of God. "Loving God is More Than a Profession," for it will lead us to do the following.

1. **Loving God will lead us to follow Him, and Him only** – "My sheep hear My voice, and I know them, and they follow Me: And I give unto them eternal life; and they shall never perish, neither shall any man pluck them out of My hand." (John 10:27-28)

2. **Loving God means doing the will of the Father** – "Not every one that saith unto Me, Lord, Lord, shall enter into the kingdom of heaven; but he that doeth the will of My Father which is in heaven." (Matthew 7:21)

3. **Lay up treasures in heaven** – "But lay up for yourselves treasures in heaven, where neither moth nor rust doth corrupt, and where thieves do not break through nor steal: For where your treasure is, there will your heart be also." (Matthew 6:20-21)

4. **Keep God's commandments** – "For this is the love of God, that we keep His commandments: and His commandments are not grievous." (I John 5:3)

5. **Love the brethren** – "If a man say, I love God, and hateth his brother, he is a liar: for he that loveth not his brother whom he hath seen, how can he love God whom he hath no seen? And this commandment have we from Him, That he who loveth God love his brother also." (I John 4:20-21)

6. **Draw nigh to God with our hearts** – "This people draweth nigh unto Me with their mouth, and honoureth Me with their lips; but their heart is far from Me." (Matthew 15:8)

7. **Deny ourselves and follow God** – "If any man will come after Me, let him deny himself, and take up his cross, and follow Me." (Matthew 16:24)

8. **Walk in the light** – "But if we walk in the light, as He is in the light, we have fellowship one with another, and the blood of Jesus Christ His Son cleanseth us from all sin." (I John 1:7)

CONCLUSION

In conclusion, our true love for God will be seen in the life that we live in this present world before men, women, and children. Our open profession of love for Jesus is important, but alone, it is not a sufficient witness of the reality of the profession. Our full submission of our heart, of our soul, of our mind, and of our strength will show by our actions that our love for Jesus is true and sincere.

"GOD IS NO RESPECTER OF PERSONS"

Text: **James 2:1-4, 8-9** – "My brethren, have not the faith of our Lord Jesus Christ, the Lord of glory, with respect of persons. For if there come unto your assembly a man with a gold ring, in goodly apparel, and there come in also a poor man in vile raiment; and ye have respect to him that weareth the gay clothing, and say unto him, Sit thou here in a good place; and say to the poor, Stand thou there, or sit here under my footstool: are ye not then partial in yourselves, and are become judges of evil thoughts? If ye fulfil the royal law according to the Scripture, Thou shalt love thy neighbour as thyself, ye do well: but if ye have respect of persons, ye commit sin, and are convinced of the law as transgressors."

INTRODUCTION

God is the God of all of humankind. He does not love any one of us more than He loves the other, and God instructs us to have the same mindset. Rank, power, and/or wealth do not influence how God deals with us, but He accepts all who fear Him and do righteousness, according to Acts 10:34-35. God uses ordinary people in great ways to accomplish great things. In times past, God, in the name of Jesus and by His Holy Spirit, washed, sanctified, and justified fornicators, idolaters, adulterers, effeminate, thieves, abusers of themselves with mankind, covetous, drunkards, revilers, and extortioners. (I Corinthians 6:9-11) Therefore, we should be careful to not rule out any one from the Kingdom of God. **"God is Not A Respecter of Persons."**

DISCUSSION

The lead text for this lesson presents a scenario that is very familiar to many of us. James, the brother of Jesus, the Christ, and leader in the church at Jerusalem, gives us a clear picture of what it means to have respect of persons. James taught Jewish Christians, who lived within Gentile communities that it would not be pleasing to God if they were to offer one who may come into their synagogue in clean apparel, well-dressed, and with a gold ring upon his finger to sit in a choice seat among the other congregants, while they offer one who is poor and who may be dressed in dirty and detestable clothing to "Stand thou there, or sit under my footstool:" (James 2:3) We must remember that the outer appearance of a person does not necessarily reveal one's inner character and destiny. God told the prophet Samuel when God sent him to the house of Jesse to make known the one who would replace Saul as king over Israel, "Look not on his countenance, or on the height of his stature; because I have refused him: for the Lord seeth not as man seeth; for man looketh on the outward appearance, but the Lord looketh on the heart." (I Samuel 16:7) Let us look at some of the persons whom God chose to use to accomplish His will in the earth.

1. **Saul** – was a diligent persecutor of the early Christians, and he was complicit in the stoning death of Stephen, whose words in defense of the Gospel of Jesus, the Christ, brought about Stephen's martyrdom. Saul thought that this new movement was blasphemous against God, and so he persecuted them. But, as he was on his way to Damascus with a letter of permission to arrest believers and transport them back to

Jerusalem, Saul encountered Jesus, and his life was forever changed. His name was changed to Paul (the Greek version of his Hebrew name, "Saul"), and he became a prolific preacher, teacher, and writer of the New Testament. **"God Is No Respecter of Persons."**

2. **Rahab** – was a prostitute, who lived in the city of Jericho. She provided both lodging and favors for travelers. She hid the two spies who were sent to Jericho by Joshua to spy out the land, when the king of Jericho came looking for them. She had heard of all that Israel's God had done on their behalf on several occasions (e.g., parting the Red Sea, destruction of Sihon, the king of the Amorites, and Og, the king of Bashan). Therefore, she greatly revered Israel's God, and she put her and her family's fate in the His hands. God honored her faith. When Joshua entered Jericho to destroy it, "...Joshua saved Rahab the harlot alive, and her father's household, and all that she had; and she dwelleth in Israel even unto this day; because she hid the messengers, which Joshua sent to spy out Jericho." (Joshua 6:25) God used this harlot to mother Boaz, who was the father of Obed through Ruth, and Obed was the father of Jesse, who was the father of David, the king. Jesus, our Lord and Savior, came through this same lineage. **"God Is No Respecter of Persons."**

3. **Jacob** – was not a common, poor man, but he lacked integrity. He was a liar, deceitful, and selfish. Nevertheless, God chose to bless the nation of Israel through Jacob. God refined Jacob's character by allowing him to go through various trials and tribulations. These experiences caused him to draw closer to God, and God established the nation of Israel through him. Out of the tribe of Judah, through one of Jacob's sons came Messiah Jesus into the world.

4. **Zacchaeus** – was a chief tax collector for the Roman Empire. The people hated tax collectors, who were also called publicans, because they caused the people to pay more taxes than were due. Tax collectors were perceived to be greedy thieves, and sinners. Yet, Jesus invited Himself to Zacchaeus' house. The people were upset that He would keep company with a sinner. But Zacchaeus was so moved by Jesus' compassion towards him that he was convicted of his sins. He repented and offered retribution to those whom he had abused. He told Jesus,

5. "Behold, Lord, the half of my goods I give to the poor; and if I have taken any thing from any man by false accusation, I restore him four-fold." (Luke 19:8) **"God Is No Respecter of Persons."**

"And such were some of you: but ye are washed, but ye are sanctified, but ye are justified in the name of the Lord Jesus, and by the Spirit of our God." (I Corinthians 6:11) **"God Is No Respecter of Persons."**

CONCLUSION

In conclusion, God has a plan and a purpose for you, as well. It neither matters what you have done, nor what it is you are currently doing. In God's own timing, and in God's own peculiar way, He will bring you to the place He wants you to be. The only thing that can hinder God's work on your behalf is your resistance and disobedience. We should remember that **"God Is No Respecter of Persons."**

"NO WEAPON FORMED AGAINST US SHALL PROSPER"

Text: **Isaiah 54:17a** – "No weapon that is formed against thee shall prosper; and every tongue that shall rise against thee in judgment thou shalt condemn. This is the heritage of the servants of the LORD, and their righteousness is of Me, saith the LORD."

INTRODUCTION

There are times when our God turns a deaf ear to us, because of sins that we continuously commit. Sin separates us from God, for God is holy. Yet, in our season of rebuke by God, He still loves us, and He longs to restore us to Himself. Even during His rebuke, His mercy still protects us in our separation from Him. Israel was in this state in our Scriptural text for this lesson. But, God told them that His punishment of them would not be forever.

DISCUSSION

It is important to remember that whatever situation or obstacle, both spiritual and physical, that is sent and meant to overtake us shall not be able to accomplish it! God's silence during Israel's time of temporary abandonment still carried with it the hope of turning their suffering into joy. The fact that God allows us to reap the consequences of our rebellion and disobedience to His will should not be construed to mean that God no longer loves us and cares for us. The Word of God is clear "Be not deceived; God is not mocked: for whatsoever a man soweth, that shall he also reap." (Galatians 6:7) In spite of their state, God wanted Israel to know that He was still in control of all aspects of their situation. The Lord God is reminding us, today, that whatsoever state we are in, He will not allow that situation to overtake us. We should remember that "God is faithful, who will not suffer you to be tempted above that ye are able; but will with the temptation also make a way to escape, that ye may be able to bear it." (I Corinthians 10:13) Therefore, we should be encouraged to know that **"No Weapon Formed Against Us Shall Prosper."**

1. **The weapons of jealousy and abuse shall not prevent you from reaching your God-ordained destiny**. Has God given you a dream, or a vision for your life? Joseph was the son of Isaac, the patriarch of the twelve tribes. He had a dream, and he shared it with his brothers. His brothers, however, were very upset about Joseph's dream, because in it, Joseph's brothers, his father, and his mother all gave honor to him as one with authority over them. His brothers sold Joseph to the Midianites, who in turn sold him to the Ishmeelites. They transported Joseph into Egypt, where he was sold to Potiphar, an officer of Pharaoh. While under Potiphar's employment, Joseph was falsely accused by Potiphar's wife, who desired to lie with Joseph. Joseph resisted, and he fled. Potiphar's wife caught Joseph's garment, and she used it as false evidence to support her claim that Joseph tried to seduce her. In spite of his situation, God was in the midst controlling and directing Joseph's life. And, God turned Joseph's mourning into joy, and he became second in command to Pharaoh in Egypt. **"No Weapon Formed Against Us Shall Prosper."**

2. **Men's mockings against you shall not prosper** – As Jesus hung on the tree at Calvary, many mocked Him saying, "He saved others; Himself He cannot save. If He be the King of Israel, let Him come down from the cross, and we will believe Him." (Matthew 27:42) Their mocking was of no effect, because even as Jesus was dying on the cross, He gained another soul for the kingdom. Two powerful principles can be gleaned from this situation. One principle is that we should not be concerned about people's opinions when they are not true, and when you know that your actions are according to the will of God. The other principle is that we should not be tempted to prove our actions to the adversaries. The onlookers challenged Jesus to prove Himself to them by coming down from the cross. They did not understand that the victory was in His dying, for Jesus could never have been permanently resurrected had He not died. The lasting victory for all of humankind was in the death, burial, and resurrection of Jesus. **"No Weapon Formed Against Us Shall Prosper."**

3. **Hold On! Your Situation is Just for a Season.** – "Weeping may endure for a night, but joy cometh in the morning." (Psalm 30:5c) Our God has the power to lift us above our situation. Hannah, one of the two wives of a man named Elkanah, was barren. Peninnah, His other wife, bore him children, and she taunted Hannah for being barren. In due season, and in God's own timing, God blessed Hannah's womb, and she conceived.

4. **You are more than a conqueror** – We need to embrace the Holy Scriptures' view of true believers. They proclaim that "If God be for us, who can be against us?" (Romans 8:31) We need not to be overly concerned about what others may say about us. We only need to be concerned about what God says about us, for our salvation is totally dependent upon Him. Therefore, let us rest assured that in every situation that arises against us "We are more than conquerors through Him that loved us." (Romans 8:37)

CONCLUSION

In this life, we will be tried and tested. It is beneficial to remember that these come to make us strong. God works all of these together for our good, as He transforms us into the image of His Son, Jesus. Let us also remember that the Lord is on our side. Therefore, **"No Weapon Formed Against Us Shall Prosper."**

"THE PRISON OF AN UNFORGIVING MINDSET"

Text: Matthew 6:14-15; Mark 11:25-26 – "For if ye forgive men their trespasses, your heavenly Father will also forgive you: but if ye forgive not men their trespasses, neither will your Father forgive your trespasses. And when ye stand praying, forgive, if ye have ought against any: that your Father also which is in heaven may forgive you your trespasses. But if ye do not forgive, neither will your Father which is in heaven forgive your trespasses."

INTRODUCTION

When we think of sin, our thoughts generally reflect on fornication, adultery, homosexuality, stealing, telling lies, murder, and the like. But, we tend to exclude an "unforgiving" mindset among our list of sins. This mindset is harmful to those who possess it, because it imprisons us. The lead text explains that the forgiveness of our sins is contingent upon our willingness to forgive others of their sins against us. Therefore, those of us who have an unforgiving mindset lock ourselves in prison, wherein only our forgiveness of others can unlock the prison doors.

DISCUSSION

Matthew, the writer of this gospel, which also bears his name, relates Jesus' teaching of God's will and intent regarding the act of forgiveness. Oftentimes we assume that we can bypass God's rules and commands by doing other good deeds. On the contrary, God means what He says. God revealed to Moses those things that He required of His chosen people, Israel, as well as those things that He requires of us even today. The events of the day may differ, however the principles of God's intent and will remain the same. Moses wrote in Deuteronomy 11:26-28, "Behold, I set before you this day a blessing and a curse; A blessing, if ye obey the commandments of the Lord your God, which I command you this day: And a curse, if ye will not obey the commandments of the Lord your God, but turn aside out of the way which I command you this day, to go after other gods, which ye have not known." We must remember that God prefers our obedience, when juxtaposed with good deeds and offerings that we may contribute. Therefore, we should not minimize Jesus' statement which says, "But if ye do not forgive, neither will your Father which is in heaven forgive your trespasses." (Mark 11:26)

Generally, no resident of a prison facility is privileged to have a key to the cell in which they reside. In a spiritual prison, the prisoner has access to the key to let him/herself out at any time. He or she only needs to make a conscious decision to obey God's command for access to the key. Failure to obey God's command will deny the prisoner access to the key that unlocks the prison door. Let us examine some ramifications of **"The Prison of An Unforgiving Mindset."**

1. **"An Unforgiving Mindset"destroys us from the inside out**. It is like a cancer that is hidden and secretly growing inside. It contaminates the body from the inside, until it is outwardly manifested thru anxiety, ill will, anger, unhappiness, etc. An unforgiving mindset becomes a breeding ground for diseases that thrive off these behaviors. We are literally killing ourselves, when we do not forgive those who have offended us. **WE** lock **OURSELVES** in prison.

2. **"An Unforgiving Mindset" hinders our prayers.** Once we are aware of God's commandment about a particular issue, we should obey that commandment. If we disobey it, we act in rebellion and pride. The Word of God tells us, "Therefore to him that knoweth to do good, and doeth it not, to him it is sin." (James 4:17) Jesus also tells us in Matthew 5:23-24, "Therefore, if thou bring thy gift to the altar, and there rememberest that thy brother hath ought against thee; Leave there thy gift before the altar, and go thy way; first be reconciled to thy brother, and then come and offer thy gift." We cannot get our prayers through to God with **"An Unforgiving Mindset,"** neither are they welcomed by God, according to Matthew 6:14-15. **WE** lock our **PRAYER LIFE** in prison.

3. **"An Unforgiving Mindset" will affect our physical condition.** Clinical studies show that an unforgiving mindset can negatively affect what we think and how we feel. These, in turn, can interrupt our bodies' natural healing process. Therefore, WE lock our HEALTH in prison.

4. **"An Unforgiving Mindset" will cause discord in our family.** When a husband will not forgive his wife; the wife will not forgive her husband; children will not forgive their parents; parents will not forgive their children; brothers & sisters will not forgive one another, the family is in discord. Our FAMILY is locked in prison.

5. **"An Unforgiving Mindset" can lead to a powerless church.** An unforgiving mindset of church members toward one another; members toward the pastor; pastor towards the members; families toward families; youth toward youth; adults toward youth; and youth against adults make a powerless church. The CHURCH is locked in prison.

6. **"An Unforgiving Mindset" can prevent our spiritual growth.** The Word of God proclaims in Galatians 6:7-9, "Be not deceived; God is not mocked: for whatsoever a man soweth, that shall he also reap." Our SPIRITUAL GROWTH is locked in prison.

7. **"An Unforgiving Mindset" can affect our present and future relationships.** Previous and present hurts, disappointments, failures, betrayals, etc., which have not been forgiven will negatively impact our relationships with others. They may cause us to be short with those whom we love, and/or they may cause us to mistrust others who may be worthy of our trust. Our **RELATIONSHIPS** are locked in prison.

8. **"An Unforgiving Mindset" reflects the stronghold of pride.** An unforgiving spirit is directly linked to pride. It feels good, especially when we have been proven to be right about the person who wronged us. This can cause us to feel justified in not forgiving that person, and we become settled and content in our decision that we will not forgive. Also, we choose to cherish the grudge and remain bitter by continually dwelling on what the person did to us. We must remember, however, "Pride goeth before destruction, and an haughty spirit before a fall." (Proverbs 16:18) Our **HUMILITY** is locked in prison.

CONCLUSION

IT IS TIME FOR A PRISON BREAK!!!! God has given us the master key that is able to unlock every situation that has us bound in prison. The master key is **"THE KEY OF FORGIVENESS."** Let us use it to set ourselves free from **"The Prison of An Unforgiving Mindset,"** and "Let all bitterness, and wrath, and anger, and clamor, and evil speaking, be put away from you, with all malice: and be ye kind one to another, tenderhearted, forgiving one another, even as God for Christ's sake hath forgiven you." (Ephesians 4:31-32) Finally, "Vengeance is mine, I will repay, saith the Lord." (Romans 12:19)

"THE BIBLE: THE STANDARD FOR RIGHTEOUS LIVING"

Text: II Timothy 3:16-17 - "All scripture is given by inspiration of God, and is profitable for doctrine, for reproof, for correction, for instruction in righteousness: That the man of God may be perfect, thoroughly furnished unto all good works."

INTRODUCTION

Our lesson today is to stress that the Bible is the only standard by which believers and those who desire to please God should live. Even though the Bible is referred to in the holy writings by several names, it is the one and selfsame book. Some familiar names by which the Bible is called include: 1) The Holy Scriptures; 2) The Living Word; 3) The Scriptures; 4) The Sword of the Spirit; 5) The Word of God; 6) The Word; and 7) The Bible.

DISCUSSION

The text for this lesson asserts that the full content of both the First and the Second Testaments are products of divine revelation and influence. It further proclaims that the whole of these writings are beneficial and helpful for **doctrine** (instruction, teaching, and learning); for **reproof** (for proving that which is right, and for conviction); for **correction** (for helping one to straighten up again); for **instruction in righteousness** (tutorage, i.e., education or training; disciplinary correction; chastening, chastisement, instruction, nurture) in (equity, which is fairness and impartiality of character, or act), according to The New Strong's Exhaustive Concordance of the Bible. It identifies the ultimate results which the Word of God is able to accomplish in us, when it is activated in our lives. It tells us that the man of God will be perfect (mature, complete), thoroughly furnished (fully equipped, prepared) to do those things that are pleasing in God's sight.

Jesus made known the tenets of righteousness to the apostles and to believers of the early church. These are written in the Bible for our knowledge, our understanding of the will of God, and for their practical application in our daily lives as children of God. The Bible records the teachings of Jesus regarding righteous living. Some of these are noted in His Sermon on the Mount, as recorded in the gospel according to Matthew, chapters 5-7. Some of Jesus' instructions for righteous living are noted below.

1. **Ye are the salt of the earth and the light of the world.** Have a positive effect upon the world, influencing the rejection of that which is morally vile; adding spice and flavor to the mundane aspects of life; and illuminating righteous living in a dark and evil world. (Matthew 5:13-14)

2. **Be swift to reconcile disagreements.** Unresolved disagreements affect our attitude towards God and our relationship with Him. Resolve disagreements quickly. (Matthew 5:23-25)

3. **Adultery is more than a physical act**. Watch those eyes, for Jesus said, "Ye have heard that it was said by them of old time, Thou shalt not commit adultery: but I say unto you, That whosoever looketh on a woman to lust after her hath committed adultery with her already in his heart." Job said, "I made a covenant with mine eyes; why then should I think upon a maid?" (Matthew 5:27-28; Job 31:1)

4. **Do not evil for evil**. God's standards are far above the standards of the world. The world says, "An eye for an eye, and a tooth for a tooth," according to Jesus. He also instructed, "That ye resist not evil: but whosoever shall smite thee on thy right cheek, turn to him the other also. Ye have heard that it hath been said, thou shalt love thy neighbor, and hate thine enemy. But I say unto you, Love your enemies, bless them that curse you, do good to them that hate you, and pray for them which despitefully use you, and persecute you; that ye may be the children of your Father which is in heaven:....." (Matthew 5:38-39; 43-45)

5. **Lay up for yourself treasures in heaven**. Many continually strive to increase their savings of money, property, and other portfolios of investments that can be stolen, misappropriated, and will be worthless in eternity to come. Jesus tells us of a better investment. "...Lay up for yourselves treasures in heaven, where neither moth nor rust doth corrupt, and where thieves do not break through nor steal; for where your treasure is, there will your heart be also." (Matthews 6:19-21).

6. **Make God and His Kingdom priorities in your life**. There is an old adage which says, "Everything's going down, but the Word of God." We are instructed, therefore, to "...Seek ye first the kingdom of God, and His righteousness; and all these things shall be added unto you. Take therefore no thought for the morrow: for the morrow shall take thought for the things of itself." (Matthew 6:33-34)

7. **Be careful in judging others**. "For with what judgment ye judge, ye shall be judged: and with what measure ye mete, it shall be measured to you again. And why beholdest thou the mote that is in thy brother's eye, but considerest not the beam that is in thine own eye? (Matthew 7:2-3)

8. **Treat others the way that you want to be treated**. "Therefore all things whatsoever ye would that men should do to you, do ye even so to them: for this is the law and the prophets." (Matthew 7:12)

9. **Choose the strait and narrow way**. "Because strait is the gate, and narrow is the way, which leadeth unto life, and few there be that find it." (Matthew 7:14)

10. **Do the will of the Father**. "Not every one that saith unto me, Lord, Lord, shall enter into the kingdom of heaven; but he that doeth the will of my Father which is in heaven." (Matthew 7:21)

CONCLUSION

We live in a world in which many have fallen away from God just as the Holy Scriptures proclaim. False teachers have caused them to denounce their God and to make void His written Word. This lesson cautions and encourages us to stand firm on the truths of the Holy Scriptures, because they are the only foundational guide to righteous living.

"THE POWER OF THE BLOOD OF JESUS"

<u>Text</u>: <u>Colossians 1:19-20a</u> – "For it pleased the Father that in Him should all fullness dwell; and, having made peace through the blood of His cross, by Him to reconcile all things unto Himself; by Him, I say, whether they be things in earth, or things in heaven."

INTRODUCTION

Blood transports oxygen, cells, proteins, hormones, and other substances throughout the body. It is also said to be essential in regulating the balance of various areas and functions of the body. Blood also has a protective function that protects us through clotting, as necessary, from excess bleeding when we are cut. Our immune system is directly related to our blood. Therefore, we can see that our Creator designed humankind in a way that its blood and its vital elements are critical to physical existence. In forbidding the killing of human beings, the Lord God explained in Leviticus 18:11 that "…the life of the flesh is in the blood: and I have given it to you upon the altar to make an atonement for your souls: for it is the blood that maketh an atonement for the soul." Therefore, the blood is not only essential to the life of the body, it is also essential for the redemption of souls, which secures eternal life with God for all who will believe. This is **"The Power of the Blood of Jesus."**

DISCUSSION

In this text, the Lord God, expands the significance of the blood to include a spiritual function and benefit. It tells us that by the cross of Jesus, the blood that He shed is sufficient to be a propitiation for the sins of humankind, as well as for the restoration of relationship between a Holy God and fallen humankind. This is **"The Power of the Blood of Jesus."** Listed below are evidences of the power of the blood of Jesus.

1. **<u>The blood fulfilled the penalty for sin</u>**. The blood of Jesus, the One who knew no sin, was sacrificed for the guilty, whose blood was infected by sin. Jesus' shed blood fulfilled the penalty for sin, which is death. "For this is My blood of the new testament, which is shed for many for the remission of sins." (Matthew 26:28)

2. **<u>The blood remits sins</u>**. "God so loved the world that He gave His only begotten Son, that whosoever believeth in Him shall not perish, but have everlasting life. Whom God hath set forth to be a propitiation through faith in His blood, to declare His righteousness for the remission of sins that are past, through the forbearance of God. And almost all things are by the law purged with blood; and without shedding of blood is no remission." (John 3:16; Romans 3:25; Hebrews 9:22).

3. **<u>The blood of Jesus provides for our healing</u>**. "But He was wounded for our transgressions, He was bruised for our iniquities: the chastisement of our peace was upon Him; and with His stripes we are healed." (Isaiah 53:5)

4. **<u>The blood of Jesus redeems from eternal damnation</u>**. Corruptible things, such as silver and gold do not have power to redeem us from sin; it was the precious blood of Jesus, a lamb without blemish. "For as much as ye know that ye were not redeemed

with corruptible things, as silver and gold, from your vain conversation received by tradition from your fathers; But with the precious blood of Christ, as of a lamb without blemish and without spot:" (I Peter 1:18-19)

5. <u>The blood purchased for God a Church</u>. Paul encouraged the elders in Ephesus to be faithful in executing their duties on behalf of the Church which Jesus purchased with His blood. "Take heed therefore unto yourselves, and to all the flock, over the which the Holy Ghost hath made you overseers, to feed the church of God, which He hath purchased with His own blood." (Acts 20:28)

<u>CONCLUSION</u>

Finally, the blood of Jesus has great power. It was shed on Calvary's cross once and for all, and it shall never lose its power. However, faith in the power of the blood of Jesus must be actively applied in our lives, if it is to accomplish all that the Word of God says is possible. Once that faith is activated, we shall be able to experience **"The Power of the Blood of Jesus."**

"THERE IS LIFE AFTER THE STORM"

<u>Text</u>: **Mark 4:37-40** - "And there arose a great storm of wind, and the waves beat into the ship, so that it was now full. And He was in the hinder part of the ship, asleep on a pillow: and they awake Him, and say unto Him, Master, carest thou not that we perish? And He arose, and rebuked the wind, and said unto the sea, Peace, be still. And the wind ceased, and there was a great calm. And He said unto them, why are ye so fearful? How is it that ye have no faith?"

INTRODUCTION

Meteorologically, and according to a Google search, the word storm means, "A violent disturbance of the atmosphere with strong winds and usually rain, thunder, lightning, and/or snow; a tumultuous reaction; an uproar, or controversy." We see from these words that a storm is a reaction that upsets the normality of a weather system. We also see that a storm may be a challenging situation that arises in our lives. I love how a leader of my church described some storms of life. He wrote, "Imagine if you woke up one day and this was your situation: You just lost your job; your home is about to be foreclosed; you are unable to feed your family and to make ends meet; your car note is three months behind; in fact, you don't park your car at home at night for fear it won't be there in the morning. To make matters worse, your son robbed the bank and killed someone. Situations arise, and sometimes they are very great. The storms in your life are ragging. You say, Lord, I can't take anymore! Where are you, God?!!! Where are you when I need you? Does God care? Does anyone care? Woe is me; I am undone. I am in a mess!"

DISCUSSION

We must remember that God has no respect of persons, and neither do the storms of life. Therefore, both the righteous and the unrighteous suffer. The main difference is that the righteous have Jesus, our Lord and Savior with us to bring us safely through every situation. If we have faith in the Word of God, we will not allow the storms in our lives to cause us to worry and to be fearful, but we will cast all of our care upon God, because He cares for us. (I Peter 5:7) In the lead text for this lesson, the disciples did not activate this principle when the storm arose on the sea. They became fearful, and they questioned whether Jesus cared that they might die. Jesus rebuked them for their lack of faith in Him. Let us put our faith in the Word of God, which says, "There hath no temptation taken you but such as is common to man: but God is faithful, who will not suffer you to be tempted above that ye are able; but will with the temptation also make a way to escape, that ye may be able to bear it." (I Corinthians 10:13)

Noted below are some things that we should remember about the storms of life.

1. <u>**Job, a righteous man, had storms.**</u> He was, according to the Scriptures, "a wealthy and upright man," who lost all of his possessions, his children, and his health. The literary style of the narrative is very dramatic. Messenger after messenger came in to give Job bad news, with each overlapping the message of the other. One servant was always left to carry the message back to Job of the onslaught of his flocks and servants. Messenger number one came in to tell Job that the Sabeans fell upon his oxen and his asses, took them away with them, and slayed all of his servants. While that servant was yet speaking, messenger number two came in to tell Job that fire fell from heaven and burned up his sheep and his servants. While

that servant was yet speaking, messenger number three came in to tell Job that the Chaldeans fell upon his camels, carried them away, and slew Job's servants. Finally, while that servant was yet speaking, messenger number four came to tell Job that his elder son's house in which his sons and daughters were celebrating was destroyed by a great wind from the wilderness. All of them were dead. These were storms in the life of Job. How did Job respond to these storms? "He arose, and rent his mantle, and shaved his head, and fell down upon the ground, and worshipped," for Job understood that he was not above suffering. He believed that **"There Was Life After the Storm,"** for God restored to Job two-fold all that he lost. (Job 1:13-22; 2:10)

2. **Storms are crises.** Can we weather the storms? Yes, we can, because it is God, who alone allows the stormy winds of pain, disappointment, failure, sickness, and disease. When we are caught in the eye of a storm, we must remember that our God is able to quiet and to calm the storm. With God on our side, we are able to endure the rage of any storm. God will show us how to be strong and to resist the enemy. The enemy must yield to the authority of Jesus' words. We have been given authority in Matthew 18:18 and II Corinthians 10:4-5, which state, "Verily I say unto you, Whatsoever ye shall bind on earth shall be bound in heaven: and whatsoever ye shall loose on earth shall be loosed in heaven," and "(For the weapons of our warfare are not carnal, but mighty through God to the pulling down of strong holds;) Casting down imaginations, and every high thing that exalteth itself against the knowledge of God, and bringing into captivity every thought to the obedience of Christ." After Jesus calmed the storm, the disciples asked, "What manner of man is this, that even the winds and the sea obey Him?" The answer, "He is King of kings, and Lord of lords!" (Mark 44:41; I Timothy 6:15)

3. **Storms should not separate us from God.** Storms should drive us closer to the true and living God, for He is our help in the midst of the storms of life. Nothing is able to separate us from the love of God, which is in Christ Jesus, our Lord. And, we should rest assured that "We are more than conquerors through Him that loved us." (Romans 8:37)

4. **Make preparation for the storms of life.** If you are not saved, get saved. Today, through this lesson, you have heard the Word of the Lord. Therefore, harden not your heart towards receiving Jesus into your life for the pardon of your sins. God is merciful, and He will forgive your sins and remember them no more. The Word of God promises that "If we confess our sins, He is faithful and just to forgive us our sins, and to cleanse us from all unrighteousness." Then, when the storms of life come, the Lord God will be with you, and He will not allow them to overtake you. "God is our refuge and strength, a very present help in trouble." (I John 1:9; Psalm 46:1)

CONCLUSION

It is not possible to live in this world and not encounter stormy days. The dramatic, emotional upheaval of a divorce, the death of a spouse, the diagnosis of a serious disease, failures, betrayals, etc., can greatly hurt us and leave scars upon the fabric of our hearts. But, Jesus is yet speaking to us through His Word, which says, "These things I have spoken unto you, that in me ye might have peace. In the world ye shall have tribulation: but be of good cheer; I have overcome the world." Remember, **"There is Life After the Storm."** (John 16:33)

"THIS IS JUST FOR A SEASON"

Text: <u>Ecclesiastes 3:1</u> - "To every thing there is a season, and a time to every purpose under the heaven:"

INTRODUCTION

In our lesson today, the word "This" is used as a pronoun to signify a specific situation, or circumstance. However, I purposely did not reveal the situation to which the subject refers, because its principle may be applied to any of the circumstances of life, both good and bad. Life has many cycles, and none of them remains forever. Can you imagine how monotonous life would be if everything remained the same every day, every week, and every year? The biblical fact that there is a time and a season for everything suggests that God does not want life to be a bore. Neither does He want us to become stagnated in our spiritual, natural, and relational growths. Therefore, He allows adversities to come into our lives. We are never left alone to deal with these, however, for God is faithful, and He has promised us, "I will never leave thee, nor forsake thee." (Hebrews 13:5)

DISCUSSION

The scriptural text for this lesson not only tells us that nothing remains the same it tells us that there is an appropriate time for the events in our lives. This text was written by King Solomon, King David's son. He inherited the kingdom after the death of his father, and he began to reign as king at a young age. The Bible proclaims that "Solomon loved the Lord." (I Kings 3:3) One night, the Lord came to Solomon in a dream, and God asked him what He should give to him. Solomon took thought of several realities before he responded to God. First, he took thought of his young age. Then, he said, "I know not how to go out or come in," which signified that he was unsure of how to be king. He also expressed concern about being king over such a great people that the Lord had chosen for Himself, and whom the Lord God had blessed to be a great multitude. Solomon's response, therefore, was a request that God would grant him "understanding to discern judgment," which by definition is wisdom. God was pleased with Solomon's request, and the request was granted. However, wisdom is of no effect until it is put into action.

Many of the decisions that were made by Solomon directly contradicted what his father had instructed and what God had commanded. In other words, he knew that which was right to do, but he chose not to do it. He lived lavishly, had hundreds of wives, and he became famous throughout the world for his great wisdom. The book of Ecclesiastes records some of Solomon's reflections on life. He warns us about the pitfalls of life, while letting us know the importance of maintaining a faithful relationship with God. In the third chapter of the book, Solomon shares general observations about life. He wants us to know that there is a season and a right time for all that happens in our lives; and that the seasons of life are not static seasons; they do change. And so, let us trust, accept, and walk in God's decisions regarding the seasons and timing for our life experiences. In so doing, let us consider the following points:

1. **Whatever you are going through in your life is just for a season.** In due time, the season you are currently in will change, just as summer gives way to fall, and fall gives way to winter, and winter gives way to spring, and night gives way to day, etc.. Life and nature are according to God's order of things.

2. **You must endure this season in order to enjoy the next.** The man Job endured his season of suffering, testing, and despair, and he was able to enjoy a season that was greater than the first. The Word of God tells us "And the LORD turned the captivity of Job…also the LORD gave Job twice as much as he had before." (Job 42:10) Job's season changed, and so will yours.

3. **A variety of seasons in our lives help to mature us in the Lord.** Neither times of joy, nor times of sorrow, last forever. Eventually, all things change. Every new day is yesterday's tomorrow. "And not only so, but we glory in tribulations also: knowing that tribulation worketh patience; and patience, experience; and experience, hope: And hope maketh not ashamed; because the love of God is shed abroad in our hearts by the Holy Ghost which is given unto us." (Romans 5:3-5)

4. **Never give up on God.** He will be there when everything else and everyone else are gone. Our trust in God and our love for Him must not be based on what He can do for us; they must be based on who God is to us. He is our Sovereign. In this season, remain faithful and committed to God in spite of the circumstances that surround you. Faith must be tried. Be encouraged by the faith of Job, who lost all that he had, but never doubted God. Job said, "…all the days of my appointed time will I wait till my change come." (Job 14:14b) "This Is Just For A Season."

5. **Trust God.** It is easy to trust God when all is well. It is not so easy to trust God when everything is falling apart, and it seems useless and unproductive to continue fighting. During these times, you must realize that you are under attack of the adversary, and the attacks may appear in various forms. The enemy wants to take you out, but God is in control. "…Be strong in the Lord, and in the power of His might. Put on the whole armour of God, that ye may be able to stand against the wiles of the devil." (Ephesians 6:10-11) Remember, "There hath no temptation taken you but such as is common to man: but God is faithful, who will not suffer you to be tempted above that ye are able; but will with the temptation also make a way to escape, that ye may be able to bear it." (I Corinthians 10:13) "This Is Just For A Season."

6. **Trust God's timing.** – Stop measuring God's timing by earthly timing. God is never late. Adjust your mindset of time to line up with God's reality of time. "…One day is with the Lord as a thousand years, and a thousand years as one day." (2 Peter 3:8.) However, you may be assured of this one thing, that whenever God answers, the answer will come at the perfect time. God is an on-time God.

CONCLUSION

Through the trying of our faith, God prepares us for the next season. Our experience of this season, our faith in God, and our dependence upon Him, will serve to draw us closer to God and to greater spiritual maturity. **"This Is Just For A Season."**

"UNDERSTANDING THE TIMES: WE NEED JESUS"

Texts: <u>2 Timothy 3:1-5</u> – "This know also, that in the last days perilous times shall come. For men shall be lovers of their own selves, covetous; boasters; proud; blasphemers; disobedient to parents; unthankful; unholy; without natural affection; trucebreakers; false accusers; incontinent; fierce; despisers of those that are good; traitors; heady; high-minded; lovers of pleasures more than lovers of God; having a form of godliness, but denying the power thereof: from such turn away."

INTRODUCTION

Today, this scripture has come alive. Many of these mindsets and behaviors have existed in past generations, but only a few times in such a perilous manner. We recall a few occasions when nations or societies reached this level, and God intervened and brought judgment upon them all. Surely, if we were to take inventory of the moral condition of the world today, we would not be able to rightly deny that we are, indeed, living in perilous times.

DISCUSSION

The Apostle Paul wrote this second letter to Timothy, his spiritual son. The contents of this letter are said to be Paul's final thoughts to Timothy, as he passed the mantle of leadership to him. In the third chapter of his letter, Paul enlightens and cautions Timothy about the things he would encounter in the future, as he leads the church. He warned him that he and other believers would be confronted with leaders who would be corrupt, seek to enlarge their own self gain, and to teach doctrines that would be out of harmony with the Gospel of Jesus Christ. Paul identified the time that would come as "the last days" and as "perilous times."

The word "**perilous**" means "terrible." Paul explained that these perilous times would be mocked with certain mindsets and behaviors. He said the people will be **covetous**, desiring that which belongs to another; they will be **boasters**, which means they will be full of pride and conceit; **proud**, which means haughty and high-minded about oneself; **blasphemers**, they will profane the name of God in every way; **unholy**, in that they will live wickedly, without fear of God; **without natural affection**, their love of family, romance, humankind, and of God will be greatly distorted and not as designed by God; **trucebreakers**, they will be untrustworthy in agreements and promises; **false accusers**, they will tell lies against others; **incontinent**, they will be without self-control in their passions, appetites, and indulgences; **fierce**, prone to violent anger; **despisers of those that are good**, they will hate those who stand for righteousness; **traitors**, they will betray others; **heady**, they will be headstrong; **high-minded**, proud and self-exalted; **having a form of godliness**, they will outwardly mimic a godly life, but they will privately live ungodly.

These are the times in which we currently live. Do any of these traits and behaviors reflect you? If your answer is "Yes," come to Jesus. He will take away all of your guilt and shame.

Run to Him; do not run away from Him. Jesus loves you, and He will forgive you. How do I know that Jesus loves you and that He will forgive you of your sins? I know that He loves you, because He died, and He made a way for the forgiveness of your sin thousands of years ago. And, not for you only, but for all who will believe and receive the gift of salvation that He has already provided.

Consider the following scriptures. Meditate on them, believe them, and receive Jesus, as your Lord and Savior.

1. "For God so loved the world, that He gave His only begotten Son, that whosoever believeth in Him should not perish, but have everlasting life." (John 3:16)
2. "But God commended His love toward us, in that, while we were yet sinners, Christ died for us." (Romans 5:8)
3. "Greater love hath no man than this, that a man lay down his life for his friends. Ye are my friends, if ye do whatsoever I command you." (John 15:13-14)
4. "For Christ also hath once suffered for sins, the just for the unjust, that He might bring us to God, being put to death in the flesh, but quickened by the Spirit:" (I Peter 1:18)
5. "If we confess our sins, He is faithful and just to forgive us our sins, and to cleanse us from all unrighteousness." (I John 1:9)
6. "He that covereth his sins shall not prosper: but whoso confesseth and forsaketh them shall have mercy." (Proverbs 28:13)
7. "In this was manifested the love of God toward us, because that God sent His only begotten Son into the world, that we might live through Him. Herein is love, not that we loved God, but that He loved us. And sent His Son to be the propitiation [the means by which our sins are forgiven] for our sins." (I John 4:9-10)
8. "And He is the propitiation for our sins: and not for ours only, but also for the sins of the whole world." (I John 2:2)
9. "Wherefore God also hath highly exalted Him, and given Him a name which is above every name: That at the name of Jesus every knee should bow, of things in heaven, and things in earth, and things under the earth; And that every tongue should confess that Jesus Christ is Lord, to the glory of God the Father." (Philippians 2:9-11)
10. "That if thou shalt confess with thy mouth the Lord Jesus, and shalt believe in thine heart that God hath raised Him from the dead, thou shalt be saved. For with the heart man believeth unto righteousness; and with the mouth confession is made unto salvation. For the scripture saith, Whosoever believeth on Him shall not be ashamed." (Romans 10:9-11)

CONCLUSION

God wants us to know that there is hope. And, that hope may be found in God's precious Son, Jesus. God loves you for He said in His Word, "As I live, saith the Lord God, I have no pleasure in the death of the wicked; but that the wicked turn from his way and live; turn ye, turn ye from your evil ways; for why will ye die, O house of Israel?" (Ezekiel 33:11) **"Understanding the Times: We Need Jesus."**

Lesson Number Twenty-Six

"WHEN YOU PRAY"

Text: **Matthew 6:5** - "And when thou prayest, thou shalt not be as the hypocrites are: for they love to pray standing in the synagogues and in the corners of the streets, that they may be seen of men. Verily I say unto you, They have their reward."

INTRODUCTION

Prayer should be an essential part of every believer's personal life and walk with God. It is not a form, or heartless communication. It should be a heartfelt and natural outreach to an awesome God, the Creator of heaven and of earth. It is the believer's mode of communication with the true and living God – the God of Abraham, the God of Isaac, and the God of Jacob.

DISCUSSION

As we study the lifestyle of our Lord and Savior, Jesus the Christ, we observe that He constantly and consistently prayed to His Father. His lifestyle was an example to us that we, too, should be in constant contact with our heavenly Father. In this very familiar scripture, Jesus is teaching on the Mount of Olives (also called Olivet in 2 Samuel 15:30 and Acts 1:12), which was, at that time, a mountain that was covered with olive trees. It was said to overlook the Old City, which is the City of David, and the Kidron Valley, land in the lower areas of hills and mountains. Jesus stood on the Mount and taught both His disciples and great multitudes of people. His teachings on prayer are part of His sermon on various other topics. This sermon is called, "The Sermon on the Mount." It begins in Matthew, chapter 5, and it ends in chapter 7. In chapter 6, Jesus gives us instructions on prayer, and these are noted below.

1. **When you pray, don't pray to impress men** - "And when thou prayest, thou shalt not be as the hypocrites are: for they love to pray standing in the synagogues and in the corners of the streets, that they may be seen of men." (Matthew 5:5) This does not mean that you should not pray in public; it means that the intent of our prayer must be honest, humble, sincere to God, and without a desire for self-exaltation, praise, and recognition from people.

2. **When you pray, do not pray long prayers that are repetitious and designed to impress others** – "But when you pray, use not vain repetitions, as the heathen do: for they think that they shall be heard for their much speaking...for your Father knoweth what things ye have need of, before ye ask Him." (Matthew 5:7; 8)

3. **When you pray, address your prayer to the Father, not to Jesus** – "After this manner therefore pray ye: Our Father which art in heaven, Hallowed be thy name." (Matthew 5:9) Jesus said, "Whatsoever ye shall ask the Father in my name, He will give it you." (John 16:23) God deals with us through our relationship with His Son, Jesus. Jesus is the believer's example. His prayers were directed to the Father, so should our prayers be directed to the Father, but in Jesus' name. It is He, who has made it possible for us to speak directly to the Father. God created us above all of His creation to have a

personal relationship with Him. Prayer allows us to approach Him, by addressing and acknowledging Him as our Father, our Creator, who loves us and cares for us.

4. **When you pray say, "Hallowed, be Thy name"** – recognize that God's name is holy and worthy of our reverence and respect. Begin to exalt Him for who He is; for His attributes; and for His character, (e.g., Lord, you are incomparable, "There is none like Thee, neither is there any God beside Thee" (2 Samuel 7:22); **God, You are the Invisible God**, "No man hath seen [You] at any time" (John 1:18); **You are All-powerful** (omnipotent), "...There is nothing too hard for Thee." (Jeremiah 32:17); **You are present everywhere at the same time** (omnipresent). "Whither shall I go from Thy spirit? or whither shall I flee from Thy presence?" (Psalm 139:7) If I ascend to the highest heights, or descend to the lowest depths, dwell in the uttermost parts of the sea, God, You are there; darkness cannot hide me, nor anyone from You (Psalm 139: 7-12); **You are all-knowing** (omniscient) – "For if our heart condemn us, God is greater than our heart, and knoweth all things." (I John 3:20)

5. **When you pray say, "Thy Kingdom come. Thy will be done in earth, as it is in heaven"** – Depicts an attitude of surrender to God's authority, and the extension of an invitation to Him to reign in us and that His will be done by us. Finally, that His ways will be reflected in the earth through us.

6. **When you pray say, "Give us this day our daily bread"** – Acknowledges that God is the source of all that we need. Thank Him for His continuous provision. As we focus on God and His righteousness, He simply adds to us the things that we need. (Matthew 6:33)

7. **When you pray say, "And forgive us our debts, as we forgive our debtors"** – Only God can forgive us of our sins. However, Jesus let us know that the forgiveness of our sins is dependent on our forgiveness of the sins of others. "For if ye forgive men their trespasses, your heavenly Father will also forgive you: But if ye forgive not men their trespasses, neither will your Father forgive your trespasses." (Matthews 6:14-15)

8. **When you pray say, "And lead us not into temptation, but deliver us from evil: For thine is the kingdom, and the power, and the glory, for ever. Amen"** – Lord, God, help us to do the right things, to make the right decisions, according to Your Holy Word, when we are tempted. We desire that our lives will bring glory and honor to Your name and not shame and condemnation. We believe that you will not allow any temptation to be more than we are able to bear. (I Corinthians 10:13)

CONCLUSION

Therefore, **"When You Pray,"** begin your prayer with **Adoration** – give God praise and honor for who He is. He is LORD over all. **Confess the sins in your life, and ask God's forgiveness**, No one can fool God. With God, things that have been done in darkness are as if they were done in broad daylight. **FIRST** forgive all who have done evil towards you that God may forgive you of your sins. **Give God thanks for all that He has done on your behalf and on behalf of others in your life and in the world.** Then, make your **Supplication/s (request/s)** unto God. Make your requests for others, then make requests for yourself. These we recommend **"When You Pray."**

"WE CAN'T HURRY GOD"

Text: **Habakkuk 2:3** - "For the vision is yet for an appointed time, but at the end it shall speak, and not lie: though it tarry, wait for it; because it will surely come, it will not tarry."

INTRODUCTION

Many of us are concerned that what the Lord God has promised us has not been manifested. The Scriptural text encourages readers of several things. It tells us that there is a time that has been set for whatever God has promised us. It reassures us that when it is the right time, God will fulfill that which He promised. It encourages us that even though the promise might be slow in coming, we should wait for it, because it will surely come to pass at God's appointed time. And, nothing shall be able to stop the vision from coming to fruition.

DISCUSSION

Our text reveals God's answer to the prophet Habakkuk's questions about God's permissive will towards the wickedness in their nation. Babylon had twice invaded Judah, and in 586 B.C. Judah was finally destroyed. This was a time of great fear, oppression, persecution, lawlessness, and immorality. But, God assured Habakkuk that though His judgment was slow in coming, it would be certain. God used the wicked nation of Babylon to chastise Judah. This did not mean that Babylon's wickedness was overlooked by God. It simply meant that He would deal with Babylon's sins in His own timing and in His own way. Waiting on God requires trusting Him, even when it seems as though everything around us is falling apart. But, we must remember that we cannot hurry God.

As we patiently wait on our break-through; on our financial blessing; on the opening of doors that God promised to open; on our healing; on the resolution of problems that seem so impossible, let us consider the following principles of this message.

1. **God has ordained for us a time and a season** - "To every thing there is a season, and a time to every purpose under the heaven: I know that whatsoever God doeth, it shall be for ever: nothing can be put to it, nor any thing taken from it: and God doeth it, that men should fear before him." (Ecclesiastes 3:1,14)

2. **The process of waiting allows us to renew our strength** - "But they that wait upon the LORD shall renew their strength; they shall mount up with wings as eagles; they shall run, and not be weary; and they shall walk, and not faint." (Isaiah 40:31) God is the source of our strength, and with Him and through Him, we can do all things.

3. **Keep on doing good** – as you wait on God. We cannot hurry God. "And let us not be weary in well doing: for in due season we shall reap, if we faint not." (Galatians 6:9)

4. **Submit every thing over to Him** – every problem, yourself, your family, your job, your marriage, even your possessions for God's control and His guidance. He can do a better job of giving us the success that we desire than we can. Let us submit to the time that He has determined to do what is best for us. "We Can't Hurry God." Therefore, "Delight thyself also in the LORD; and He shall give thee the desires of thine heart." (Psalm 37:4) "The Lord is not slack concerning His promise, as some men count slackness; but is longsuffering to us-ward..." (2 Peter 39a). Therefore, know that when God answers, He will always be right on time.

5. **God is the God of time** – It will never be too late for God to do what He has promised to do for us. "But, beloved, be not ignorant of this one thing, that one day is with the Lord as a thousand years, and a thousand years as one day." (2 Peter 3:8) David recognized that time is in God's hands. In Psalm 31:15, he proclaims "My times are in Thy hand: deliver me from the hand of mine enemies, and from them that persecute me." God knows when it's time to bring us out; when it's time to deliver us; and when it is time to give us that blessing.

6. **He's preparing you for the blessing** – No matter what may be going wrong in our life, it cannot prevent us from getting to the place God is taking us. His delay signifies that the time is not yet, although we might not agree with that analogy. Joseph was the eleventh son of Jacob; the first of Rachel, Jacob's wife who was barren for many years. God gave Joseph a peak at his future when he was around seventeen years of age. God showed him that he would be a great leader, and that his father, mother, brothers, and all of his kindred would be subject to him and give him honor. This, of course, did not sit well with any of these. The vision took many years, and Joseph suffered much pain on his way to his destiny, but he reached his destiny. We, too, shall reach our destiny.

CONCLUSION

In conclusion, let us remember that "We Can't Hurry God." We have to wait on Him. And, as we wait, we must exemplify trust in Him. Time and experience have shown that He may not come when we want Him to come, but He will be right on time. "And we know that all things work together for good to them that love God, to them who are the called according to His purpose." (Romans 8:28) Therefore, every adversity, every struggle, every sickness, every stumbling block that may come our way should be viewed and used as stepping stones to lift us up out of these circumstances and propel us to our destiny.

"BE STEADY IN THIS UNSTEADY WORLD"

Text: <u>I Corinthians 15:58</u> – "Therefore, my beloved brethren, be ye stedfast, unmoveable, always abounding in the work of the Lord, forasmuch as ye know that your labour is not in vain in the Lord."

INTRODUCTION

This lesson focuses on how to remain with a faithful, encouraged. and consistent mindset in the midst of troubles, relationship challenges, family confrontations, doubts, fears, challenges in our health, the unfaithfulness of others, etc. I call this state of mind "steady," in this lesson. Some may feel that this is a hard proposition because of the perverse and evil world in which we live. While being steady in our resolve and commitment to live holy in this present world is, indeed, a challenge, it can be accomplished by those who remain in close, intimate relationship with God.

DISCUSSION

In the lead text for this lesson, the Apostle Paul teaches the principles of the resurrection of the body by clearly delineating the differences between the natural and the spiritual bodies. He makes a convincing argument that the spiritual body is the most important of the two bodies, because it will give us the victory over everything that is natural, corrupt, and mortal; only that which is spiritual shall be of everlasting benefit to us. All that we do for the Lord, and on behalf of His kingdom, shall eternally benefit us in this world and in the world to come.

Jesus told His disciples in John 14:2-3, as He prepared them for His death, burial, and resurrection, "In my Father's house are many mansions: if it were not so, I would have told you. I go to prepare a place for you. And if I go and prepare a place for you, I will come again, and receive you unto Myself; that where I am, there ye may be also." This promise is to us today, as dear followers of Jesus. But we must endure hardships and disappointments with our hope intact. We must be steady, and let nothing dissuade us in our faithful service unto the Lord and to the world. Therefore, we are called to be "stedfast and unmoveable, always abounding in the work of the Lord....," and we are reassured with the final words of the text which say, "...forasmuch as ye know that your labour is not in vain in the Lord." (I Corinthians 15:58) The word "steady" means to be "constant, stable, and unchanging," according to <u>Merriam-Webster's Dictionary and Thesaurus</u>. This same source says that the word "unmoveable" means "incapable of being moved; firmly fixed."

To **"Be Steady in This Unsteady World"** this can be done only when we remember that the situation or challenge at-hand is not ours to fight; it is the Lord's. The Lord God sent a message to Jehoshaphat, king of the tribe of Judah, and all the people of Jerusalem, when they were confronted with threats of battle from the children of Moab, Ammon, and others of the region who joined in with them to fight against Judah. The Lord God instructed, "Be not afraid nor dismayed by reason of this great multitude; for the battle is not yours, but God's. Ye shall not need to fight in this battle: set yourselves, stand ye still, and see the salvation of the LORD with you, O Judah and Jerusalem: fear not, nor be dismayed; tomorrow go out against them: for the LORD will be with you." (2 Chronicles 20:15-17) Our trust must be in God; not in ourselves.

Give Him the reins; He is the best navigator to get us through onto the other side. Noted below are some things that we can do to **"Be Steady in This Unsteady World,"** especially when all hope is gone and everything seems to be falling apart.

1. <u>**Trust God**</u>. "Rest in the LORD, and wait patiently for Him: fret not thyself because of him who prospereth in his way, because of the man who bringeth wicked devices to pass." (Psalm 37:7) He is in control of every situation of life, and He "will not suffer you to be tempted above that ye are able; but will with the temptation also make a way to escape, that ye may be able to bear it." (I Corinthians 10:13)

2. <u>**Fight a good fight, finish our course, and keep the faith**</u>. This suggests that we must endure all of life's challenges until the end and finish the assignment the Lord God has given to each of us, without compromising the faith which we received and do believe. The Apostle Paul proclaimed, when he knew his life was near the end, "For I am now ready to be offered, and the time of my departure is at hand. I have fought a good fight, I have finished my course, I have kept the faith:" (2 Timothy 4:6-7)

3. <u>**Overcome the world**</u>. "...Be not conformed to this world: but be ye transformed by the renewing of your mind, that ye may prove what is that good, and acceptable, and perfect, will of God. Be sober, be vigilant; because your adversary the devil, as a roaring lion, walketh about, seeking whom he may devour: Whom resist stedfast in the faith, knowing that the same afflictions are accomplished in your brethren that are in the world." (Romans 12:2; I Peter 5:8-9)

4. <u>**Hold fast to sound biblical teachings**</u>. Do not allow the false teachings of this world to cause you to be unstable. Paul cautioned Timothy in his last letter to him that he should be watchful of teachings that were contrary to that which he had received. Paul told Timothy, "For the time will come when they will not endure sound doctrine; but after their own lusts shall they heap to themselves teachers, having itching ears; And they shall turn away their ears from the truth, and shall be turned unto fables. But watch thou in all things, endure afflictions, do the work of an evangelist, make full proof of thy ministry." (2 Timothy 4:3-5)

5. <u>**Recognize that God is the Source of our strength**</u>. Continually remind yourself, "I can do all things through Christ, Who strengtheneth me." (Philippians 4:13) Jesus reminded Paul, "My grace is sufficient for thee: for My strength is made perfect in weakness." (2 Corinthians 12:9)

6. <u>**We are not alone. Jesus is with us in our situations**</u>. "And, behold there arose a great tempest in the sea, insomuch that the ship was covered with the waves: but He was asleep. And His disciples came to Him, and awoke Him, saying, Lord, save us: we perish. And He saith unto them, 'Why are ye fearful, O ye of little faith?' Then He arose, and rebuked the winds and the sea; and there was a great calm." (Matthew 8:24-26)

<u>CONCLUSION</u>

If we are going to **"Be Steady in This Unsteady World,"** we must increase our patience, and stand firm on our faith in God and on His promises, as we wait on Him to bring us through. Finally, let us remember that there is nothing too hard for our God.

"FAITH THAT WORKS"

Text: Genesis 12:1-4 – "Now the Lord had said unto Abram, Get thee out of thy country, and from thy kindred, and from thy father's house, unto a land that I will shew thee: And I will make of thee a great nation, and I will bless thee, and make thy name great; and thou shalt be a blessing: And I will bless them that bless thee, and curse him that curseth thee: and in thee shall all families of the earth be blessed. So Abram departed, as the Lord had spoken unto him;...."

INTRODUCTION

This lesson is entitled, **"Faith That Works,"** because it focuses on the importance of putting our faith into action. The Bible says, "Faith is the substance of things hoped for, the evidence of things not seen." (Hebrews 11:1). The word "faith" is the Greek word hupostasis (hoop-os'-stas-is), according to Strong's Concordance to the King James Version of the Bible. When we consider the "substance" of that for which we have hope, we make reference to the very "essence" of that thing. The "very essence," in turn, may be understood as the "essential nature," which is the "fundamental nature or quality; and the physical material from which something is made or has its discreet existence," according to Merriam-Webster's Dictionary and Thesaurus. A review of synonyms for the word "essence" includes words such as, "nature, soul, stuff, substance, heart, and spirit." I especially liked the word, "stuff."

These explanations of faith and its essence inform us that faith is the stuff, or natural composition of the thing for which we hope. For example, if we desire an apple, faith is as the seed of the apple. The red or green fruit, with its sweet or tart taste; the crispy, juicy, and off-white pulp; as well as its nutrients of Vitamin C, beta-carotene, and B-complex vitamins, flavonoids, and tartic acid are all within the seed, although they are not yet manifested. Everything that the apple will be after it is fully grown is present in the seed. Likewise, faith is the seed (essence, substance) of the thing that we desire, even though it is not yet visible. But, in due time, and according to God's will, it will be manifested.

DISCUSSION

"Faith That Works" is faith that is put into action, before any evidence or reassurance that what is desired, or has been promised, is manifested. The man, Abram, was very rich in livestock. He was the husband of Sarai and the son of a man named Terah. The text for this lesson tells us that the Lord God spoke to Abram. He instructed him to leave his country, his relatives, and his father's house, and to go to a land that God did not call by name. Then, God made a series of promises to Abram that were contingent upon his obedience to God's commands. These promises included the following: 1) Abram would be the father of a great nation; 2) God would bless him; 3) God would make his name great; 4) Abram would be a blessing; 5) God would bless them that bless Abram; 6) God would curse them that curse Abram; and 6) in Abram shall all families of the earth be blessed. Then, we are told that "Abram departed." (Genesis 12:4) Abram's obedience illustrated **"Faith That Works,"** because he did as the Lord God directed, without knowing his destination, and without seed to make himself a great nation. All of God's promises were wrapped up in Abram's move of faith. They were not yet manifested, but in the spirit realm, these blessings already existed. And, in God's timing, they were unleashed to Abram and to his seed.

Listed below are more encouraging thoughts on **"Faith That Works."**

1. **"Faith That Works" obeys God and trusts Him at His Word.** His Word reassures us, and proclaims, "For as the rain cometh down, and the snow from heaven, and returneth not thither, but watereth the earth, and maketh it bring forth and bud, that it may give seed to the sower, and bread to the eater: So shall My word be that goeth forth out of My mouth: it shall not return unto Me void, but it shall accomplish that which I please, and it shall prosper in the thing whereto I sent it." (Isaiah 55:10-11)

2. **"Faith That Works" does not waiver.** To waiver hinders the fulfillment of the thing that has been promised. The Word of God tells us, "But let him ask in faith, nothing wavering. For he that wavereth is like a wave of the sea driven with the wind and tossed. For let not that man think that he shall receive any thing of the Lord. A double minded man is unstable in all his ways." (James 1:6-8)

3. **"Faith That Works" is firmly rooted in Jesus.** Our faith must not be in that which we are able to accomplish, neither in the abilities of others. It must be totally in Jesus. When the storms arise, and the winds begin to blow, Jesus can calm the storms in our lives. "And He saith unto them, Why are ye fearful, O ye of little faith? Then He arose, and rebuked the winds and the sea; and there was a great calm." (Matthew 8:26)

4. **"Faith That Works" moves to fulfill God's will in the earth and for others.** God uses us to carry out His will in the earth; to bless others; to assist others; to encourage others; to provide for others. The Lord God prompted James to ask us a question in the epistle that bears his name, "What doth it profit, my brethren, though a man say he hath faith, and have not works? can faith save him?" (James 2:14) Then, James goes on to explain, "If a brother or sister be naked, and destitute of daily food, And one of you say unto them, Depart in peace, be ye warmed and filled; notwithstanding ye give them not those things which are needful to the body; what doth it profit? Faith is made perfect by our works." (James 2:15-16, 22)

CONCLUSION

In conclusion, **"Faith That Works"** has power to change shortcomings, testings, and disappointments into praises and thanksgivings unto God. Rahab, a harlot in Jericho at the time Joshua sent spies into the city, put her faith in the God of Israel, who had done so many wonderful things on Israel's behalf. She helped the spies to escape those who sought to kill them, with anticipation that they would show favor to her and her family upon their return to destroy the city. That for which she hoped became reality, because she acted in faith to save the spies. Rahab exemplified **"Faith That Works."**

"TOMORROW MIGHT BE TOO LATE"

Text: **Luke 16:22-23** - "And it came to pass, that the beggar died, and was carried by the angels into Abraham's bosom: the rich man also died, and was buried; And in hell he lift up his eyes, being in torments, and seeth Abraham afar off, and Lazarus in his bosom."

INTRODUCTION

In the twenty-fourth chapter of the Gospel According to St. Matthew, the disciples of Christ Jesus asked Him, "Tell us, when shall these things be? And what shall be the sign of thy coming, and of the end of the world?" (Matthew 24:3) Jesus later replied, after He had given several examples of happenings prior to the last days and His Second Coming, "But of that day and hour knoweth no man, no, not the angels of heaven, but my Father only." (Matthew 24:36) In other words, the time is known to no one, except the Father. Therefore, the underlying principle for the subject of this lesson is that true believers and all who desire to send eternity in heaven with God should not delay in lining themselves up with God's will and God's ways, since no one knows when Jesus will come again as our Judge. I suggest that you read the full story of the Rich man and Lazarus, which is found in Luke 16:19-31. It is important to note that it will be too late for all who die prior to His return and who do not have a personal relationship with God. This lesson is to sound the alarm that **"Tomorrow Might Be Too Late."**

DISCUSSION

The narrative in our scriptural text for this lesson relates the story of a man who waited too late. He was a rich man, who lived lavishly in his lifetime. Oftentimes, we tend to not worry about, or even to consider tomorrow when all is well. This is especially so, when we have no financial woes, and we are able to do all that we desire, whenever we desire to do it. The rich man in this text was in such a position.

A beggar named Lazarus was placed outside of the gate of the rich man's dwelling place. Lazarus merely desired the "crumbs which fell from the rich man's table," according to verse twenty-one. The text does not tell us that the rich man was aware of Lazarus' presence at his gate, but it is inferred. It is further inferred that the rich man made no effort to help the beggar, nor did he do anything to assist the beggar when he had the opportunity. The text does not tell us how long Lazarus was lain at the rich man's gate before Lazarus died. But, the times that he was there were opportunities for the rich man to show compassion towards Lazarus by providing him food, giving him shelter, and providing medical care for the sores that were upon his body. The rich man did nothing. Eventually, Lazarus died, and the Scripture proclaims in verse twenty-two that he "was carried by the angels into Abraham's bosom." His personal state was immediately changed. It reminds us of the book of Revelation, chapter twenty-one, verse four, wherein we are given a visible picture of life, as it shall be, in the heavenly city. "And God shall wipe away all tears from their eyes; and there shall be no more death, neither sorrow, nor crying, neither shall there be any more pain: for the former things are passed away."

Then, we are told in our lead text that "The rich man also died, and was buried; And in hell he lift up his eyes, being in torments, and seeth Abraham afar off, and Lazarus in his bosom. And he cried and said, Father Abraham, have mercy on me, and send Lazarus, that he may dip the tip of his finger in water, and cool my tongue; for I am tormented in this flame. But Abraham said, Son, remember that thou in thy lifetime receivedst thy good things, and likewise Lazarus evil things: but now he is comforted, and thou art tormented. And beside all this, between us and you there is a great gulf fixed: so that they which would pass from hence to you cannot; neither can they pass to us, that would come from thence." (Luke 16:22-26) The last time that the rich man passed Lazarus without helping him, was the rich man's last opportunity to do the right thing regarding Lazarus. Tomorrow for the rich man was too late.

Listed below are some points from the lesson that we should consider:

1. **Do not ignore opportunities to make a difference in someone's life**, because **"Tomorrow Might Be Too Late."** Every time the rich man passed the beggar at his gate and did nothing to help him, he missed opportunities to make life-changing differences in the beggar's life. The Word of God says, "But whoso hath this world's goods, and seeth his brother have need, and shutteth up his bowels of compassion from him, how dwelleth the love of God in him." (I John 3:17)

2. **Your hour will come as a thief in the night**, and **"Tomorrow Might Be Too Late."** The rich man did not expect to die when he died. Therefore, he did not have time to reconsider his response to Lazarus' request. The Word proclaims, "...If therefore thou shalt not watch, I will come on thee as a thief, and thou shalt not know what hour I will come upon thee." (Revelation 3:3)

3. **Have mercy on the poor and needy**, for **"Tomorrow Might Be Too Late."** Jesus explained that when He returns in His glory, He will separate the sheep from the goats. At that time, the sheep will be invited to inherit the kingdom that was prepared for them from the beginning. The sheep are described as those who showed compassion on the needy by meeting their needs. Jesus said, "For I was an hungred, and ye gave me meat: I was thirsty, and ye gave me drink: I was a stranger, and ye took me in: Naked, and ye clothed me: I was sick, and ye visited me: I was in prison, and ye came unto me." (Matthew 25:35-36)

4. **Family inheritance will not be sufficient to get you into the kingdom.** After the rich man died, and he was in torment in hell, "He cried and said, Father Abraham, have mercy on me, and send Lazarus, that he may dip the tip of his finger in water, and cool my tongue; for I am tormented in this flame. But Abraham said, Son, remember that thou in thy lifetime receivedst thy good things, and likewise Lazarus evil things: but now he is comforted, and thou art tormented." (Luke 16:24-25) Jesus said, "Not every one that saith unto me, Lord, Lord, shall enter into the kingdom of heaven; but he that doeth the will of my Father which is in heaven." (Matthew 7:21)

CONCLUSION

The moral of this lesson is that we must be careful as to the way we respond to situations that confront us. Our delay in a proper response, as well as our incorrect response, could jeopardize our eternal destination, and **"Tomorrow Might Be Too Late."** Finally, Jesus reminds us, "...Behold I come quickly; and my reward is with me, to give every man according as his work shall be." (Revelation 22:12)

"I WILL BE CONTENT"

Text: Philippians 4:11; Acts 16:22 – "Not that I speak in respect of want: for I have learned, in whatsoever state I am, therewith to be content. And at midnight Paul and Silas prayed, and sang praises unto God: and the prisoners heard them."

INTRODUCTION

David proclaimed in Psalm 34:1, "I will bless the Lord at all times: His praise shall continually be in my mouth." We know from the Scriptures that David suffered greatly, because of his sins. Yet, in the midst of his suffering, he said that he would bless the Lord at all times, which meant in the good times, as well as in the not-so-good times. We must remember that God neither loses His power, nor diminishes His strength because of our troubles. The writer of Hebrews 13:15 says that we should "...offer the sacrifice of praise to God continually, that is, the fruit of our lips giving thanks to His name." We will be able to do these things only when we WILL in our minds and in our hearts to be content, which means that we make conscious determinations that we will not be overly concerned about our negative situation. The Word proclaims, "The righteous cry and the Lord heareth and delivereth them out of all their troubles (Psalm 34:17); and that "The angel of the Lord encampeth round about them that fear Him, and delivereth them." (34:7) The Word of God further proclaims that "Many are the afflictions of the righteous: but the Lord delivereth him out of them all" (Psalm 34:19).

DISCUSSION

The lead text of Philippians is taken from one of Apostle Paul's four prison epistles. These letters are said to have been written while Paul was under house arrest at Rome. Notice that Paul yet had the mind to encourage the saints who were physically free. The other three prison epistles of the Second Testament include Ephesians, Colossians, and Philemon. The letters to the Philippians, the Ephesians, and the Colossians were penned specifically for the saints at Philippi, Ephesus, and Colossae, while the epistle of Philemon was specifically addressed to a Christian slave owner named Philemon. Paul never stopped sharing the Gospel with others, even in his suffering. We need that same resolve, which says, "I Will Be Content" in whatsoever situation that I find myself.

The situation in Acts 16:22 which led to Paul and Silas' imprisonment taught Paul the benefits of being content in the midst of suffering and trouble. They were imprisoned for casting out a demon of divination from a certain damsel, whose gift brought her masters much gain. They brought Paul and Silas before the magistrates, and they accused them of causing great trouble in their city by teaching customs that were unlawful to them as Romans. They tore off Paul's and Silas' clothes, beat them with many stripes, and cast them into prison. Verse 25 tells us that "At midnight Paul and Silas prayed, and sang praises unto God: and the prisoners heard them."

The word "content" in this lesson text is the Greek word "<u>autarkes</u>" (ow-tar'-kace), which means "Self-complacent." The word complacent means "satisfied" with who you are, and what you are (in Christ Jesus). Paul was satisfied with who he was in Christ Jesus, and He trusted Christ to be there with him and for him. He was content to know that God was still in full control. Let us also resolve to be content in whatever state we are find ourselves, knowing that our God is able to come to our rescue. Let us look at instances of Paul's resolve to be content.

1. **"I Will Be Content," even in bodily affliction**. Paul recounted that "...There was given to me a thorn in the flesh, the messenger of Satan to buffet me, lest I should be exalted above measure. For this thing I besought the Lord thrice that it might depart from me." (2 Corinthians 12:7b-8) But, Jesus told Paul, "My grace is sufficient for thee: for My strength is made perfect in weakness." (2 Corinthians 12:9b) Paul responded, "Most gladly therefore will I rather glory in my infirmities, that the power of Christ may rest upon me. Therefore, I take pleasure in infirmities, in reproaches, in necessities, in persecutions, in distresses for Christ's sake: for when I am weak, then am I strong." (2 Corinthians 12:9c-10)

2. **"I Will Be Content," when I am bitten by a venomous snake**. Paul was literally bitten by a poisonous snake during a travel stop at an island called Melita. The indigenous people anxiously looked on, awaiting Paul's immediate demise. They assumed that Paul must be a "murderer, whom, though he hath escaped the sea, yet vengeance suffereth not to live." (Acts 28:4) But Paul "shook off the beast into the fire, and felt no harm." (v. 5) Choose to be content, and shake off the attacks of the enemy that are intended to destroy you.

3. **"I Will Be Content," when I am falsely accused, and the enemy wants to kill me**. "In Damascus, the governor, under Aretas the king, kept the city of the Damascenes with a garrison, desirous to apprehend me: And through a window in a basket was I let down by the wall, and escaped his hands." Our God makes ways out of no way.

4. **"I Will Be Content," when my life seems to be headed for shipwreck on a stormy sea**. When it seems that all hope of your making it through the storm is lost, listen to God's leading and His reassurance. God sent an angel to reassure Paul that they would arrive safely through the storm. (Acts 27:23-25)

CONCLUSION

Therefore, in spite of your circumstances, and all that you may be going through, say to yourself, **"I Will Be Content,"** for I have the blessed assurance that God loves me, and He cares for me. He has promised to never leave me, nor to forsake me. I choose to trust Him at His word, and **"I Will Be Content,"** and as the Scriptures say, "Giving thanks always for all things unto God and the Father in the name of our Lord Jesus Christ."(Ephesians 5:20) Finally, let us remember "...Godliness with contentment is great gain." (I Timothy 6:6)

"BY ONE MAN"

Text: **Romans 5:12, 15b** – "Wherefore, as by one man sin entered into the world, and death by sin; and so death passed upon all men, for that all have sinned: For if through the offence of one many be dead, much more the grace of God, and the gift by grace, which is by one man, Jesus Christ, hath abounded unto many."

INTRODUCTION

Today's lesson is to remind us of the power that is within each of us. One person can negatively or positively impact one's life, the lives of their children and family members, their friends, and institutions with which they are connected, etc. "By One Man" a war of nations can be started. "By One Man," families can be torn apart. "By One Man," friendships can be strained, and even severed.

DISCUSSION

"By One Man," the man, Adam, the whole of humankind was negatively affected. Adam's charge was to obey God by not eating from the tree of the knowledge of good and evil. His choice to disobey God was met with severe consequences upon them and all of humankind. Yet, God was merciful towards Adam and Eve, and he did not allow the disobedience of one man to end His will for humankind and their future. God sent another man, the Man Jesus, to take away the penalty and the stain of Adam's sin. He also made it possible for us to restore our individual relationship with God through His total obedience to the will of the Father.

Listed below are reflections of all that God has done "By One Man."

1. **By One Man, Adam** – "…sin entered into the world, and death by sin; (Romans 5:12)
2. **By One Man, Adam** – "…death passed upon all men, for that all have sinned:" (Romans 5:12)
3. **By One Man, Adam** – "…death reigned from Adam to Moses, even over them that had not sinned after the similitude of Adam's transgression, who is the figure of Him that was to come." (Romans 5:14)
4. **By One Man, Adam** – "…many be dead…." (Romans 5:15)
5. **By One Man, Adam** – "…judgment came upon all men to condemnation." (Romans 5:18)
6. **By One Man, Adam** – "There is none righteous, no, not one. There is none that understandeth, there is none that seeketh after God. They are all gone out of the way, they are together become unprofitable; there is none that doeth good, no, not one." (Romans 3:10-12)

"But God, who is rich in mercy, for His great love wherewith He loved us, even when we were dead in sins, hath quickened us together with Christ, (by grace ye are saved;) And hath raised us up together, and made us sit together in heavenly places in Christ Jesus: That in the ages to come He might shew the exceeding riches of His grace in His kindness toward us through Christ Jesus."(Ephesians 2:4-7) Therefore, **"By One Man,"** God also performed the following.

1. **By One Man, Jesus** – "If we confess our sins, He is faithful and just to forgive us our sins, and to cleanse us from all unrighteousness." (I John 1:9)
2. **By One Man, Jesus** – "...God commendeth His love toward us, in that, while we were yet sinners, Christ died for us." (Romans 5:8)
3. **By One Man, Jesus** – "...the grace of God, and the gift of grace, which is by one man, Jesus Christ, hath abounded unto many." (Romans 5:15)
4. **By One Man, Jesus** – "Knowing this, that our old man is crucified with Him, that the body of sin might be destroyed, that henceforth we should not serve sin. For he that is dead is freed from sin." (Romans 6:6-7)
5. **By One Man, Jesus** – "...being justified by faith, we have peace with God through our Lord Jesus Christ." (Romans 5:1)
6. **By One Man, Jesus** – ""God sending His own Son in the likeness of sinful flesh, and for sin, condemned sin in the flesh: And by Him all that believe are justified from all things, from which ye could not be justified by the law of Moses." (Romans 8:3; Acts 13:39)

CONCLUSION

In conclusion, it is clear that **"By One Man"** sin, death, condemnation, and separation from God came upon all of humankind. But, it is also clear that righteousness, forgiveness, eternal life with God, and a restored relationship with Him was also **"By One Man."** By Adam, sin came upon all of humankind; but by Jesus, the penalty for sin was paid. And, now all who believe and receive Jesus as Lord and Savior may now have hope, assurance of salvation, and eternal life with God.

"RESTORE ME"

Text: **Psalm 51:7-12** – "Create in me a clean heart, O God; and renew a right spirit within me. Cast me not away from Thy presence; and take not Thy holy spirit from me. Restore unto me the joy of Thy salvation; and uphold me with Thy free spirit."

INTRODUCTION

The subject of this lesson is a direct request to Almighty God in recognition that only He can create in us a clean heart, renew a right spirit within us, restore in us the joy of His salvation, and uphold us with His free Spirit.. God is the designer and creator of humankind. And, although He has given knowledge and skills to medical doctors, scientists, pharmaceutical companies, etc. to repair, care for, and to maintain the health of our minds and bodies, we realize that the ability to heal, to give life, and to allow death are still under God's sovereign control.

The word "restore" means, according to a Google search, to "bring back (a previous right, practice, custom, or situation); reinstate; reimpose; reinstall; reestablish; to return (someone or something) to a former condition, place, or position. This is the situation in which David, the author of this psalm, found himself at its writing. David was in need of restoration to a right relationship with God.

DISCUSSION

Psalm 51, a psalm of David, the King of Israel, is a psalm of penitence. This means that it is "the action of feeling or showing sorrow and regret for having done wrong," as noted in Google. When we truly love God, it is literally impossible for us to commit sin without feeling sorry for displeasing God. However, while we are in the midst of sinning, many have a tendency to suppress these feelings of remorse, and we continue to please the flesh at almost any cost. From his roof, David saw a woman bathing herself, and he lusted after her. The epistle of James tells us in 1:15 that "...When lust hath conceived, it bringeth forth sin: and sin, when it is finished, bringeth forth death." David did not die a physical death, but he experienced a separation from God's presence with sadness and remorse. After he committed adultery with Bathsheba, the wife of one of his faithful soldiers, David found himself trying to cover up this sin by committing other sins.

In spite of his failures, David is styled as a man after God's own heart. The tone of the Holy Scriptures presents an overall picture of David as a flawed individual whose sins were not covered over, but they were publicly uncovered and punished. Nevertheless, he was still a man of God who truly loved God and who was faithful to God's Law.

It is good to know that God knows our hearts, especially when our actions do not line up with the intents of our hearts. I Samuel 16:7 tells us that "...The Lord said unto Samuel, Look not on his countenance, or on the height of his stature; because I have refused him: for the Lord seeth not as a man seeth; for man looketh on the outward appearance, but the Lord looketh on the heart." However, because sin that has not been confessed and forgiven separates us from the Presence of the Lord, David found himself in need of restoration. In order for him to once again feel God's Presence and to have fellowship with Him, David needed to come clean with God, ask for forgiveness, and endure the consequences that were sure to come. A review of David's penitent behavior, gives us a glimpse of at least six things we can do, as we seek God's restoration.

1. **Ask God for mercy.** David said, "Have mercy upon me, O God, according to thy lovingkindness: according unto the multitude of thy tender mercies blot out my transgressions." (Psalm 51:1)

2. **Acknowledge that you need to be washed.** "Wash me thoroughly from mine iniquity, and cleanse me from my sin. (Psalm 51:2)

3. **Confess that you have sinned.** "For I acknowledge my transgressions: and my sin is ever before me." (Psalm 51:3)

4. **Realize that your sins were actually against God.** "Against thee, thee only, have I sinned...." (Psalm 51:4a)

5. **Ask God for a clean heart and a right spirit.** "Create in me a clean heart, O God; and renew a right spirit within me." (Psalm 51:10)

6. **Ask God to restore your joy.** "Restore unto me the joy of thy salvation; and uphold me with thy free spirit." (Psalm 51:12)

7. **God desires that you do not perish.** "For God hath not appointed us to wrath, but to obtain salvation by our Lord Jesus Christ, Who died for us, that, whether we wake or sleep, we should live together with Him." (I Thessalonians 5:9-10)

8. **Let God lead you.** "And the Lord direct your hearts into the love of God, and into the patient waiting for Christ." (II Thessalonians 3:5)

CONCLUSION

David humbled himself, and he became very sorrowful after God exposed his sins to the prophet, Nathan. God instructed Nathan to go to David and to ask him,. "Wherefore hast thou despised the commandment of the LORD, to do evil in His sight?" Then, God told Nathan to expose to David the evils that he had done in God's sight. We should remember that Jesus proclaimed, "For nothing is secret, that shall not be made manifest; neither any thing hid, that shall not be known and come abroad." (Luke 8:17) Sin has consequences. It may be forgiven, but the consequences must come. Nevertheless, we have hope in Jesus, who, by way of the cross, has made a way of restoration for our souls. Therefore, "... we know that all things work together for good to them that love God, to them who are the called according to His purpose." (Romans 8:28) David was restored. And now, Lord, **"Restore Me."**

"GET ANCHORED IN THE TRUTH AND STAND ON HIM"

Text: **John 14:5-6** – "Thomas saith unto him, Lord, we know not whither thou goest; and how can we know the way? Jesus saith unto him, 'I am the way, the truth, and the life: no man cometh unto the Father, but by me."

INTRODUCTION

We are living in a time wherein that which was once accepted as truth is now being challenged as untrue. Truth is becoming relative to one's own interpretation and understanding, which suggests that truth is changeable and that it is directly dependent upon the situations. These theories and suppositions are deceptions of the adversary and his agents to lead the nation and believers away from the eternal God, and to cause division and confusion among us. Jesus personalized the Truth when He said, "I am the Truth."

DISCUSSION

We recognize that our Creator has designed the world with a system of opposites. For example, in this world, there is hot, and there is cold; there is happy and there is sad; there is up and there is down; and there is good, and there is evil. Yet, the enemy seeks to convince us today that there is no truth, neither are there lies. Merriam-Webster describes truth as "Honesty; the real state of things; fact; the body of real events or facts; actuality." But a review of our text for this lesson reflects that Jesus proclaimed that He is the Way, the Truth, and the Life. The question then arises, How is Jesus the Truth?

The Holy Scriptures proclaim in the Gospel According to John 1:1-2 that "In the beginning was the Word, and the Word was with God, and the Word was God. The same was in the beginning with God." In verse fourteen, John tells us that this same Word became flesh, and He resided among the disciples and others. John says that they witnessed the Word's glory, which was reflective of glory that only one who was begotten of God could possess. The begotten was "full of grace and truth," according to John. Therefore, Jesus is the Truth upon Whom we must anchor ourselves. The Apostle John shares his personal testimony regarding his knowledge of Jesus' identity. He tells us in the Gospel that he penned and which also carries his name, "...I saw the Spirit descending from heaven like a dove, and it abode upon Him. And I knew Him not: but He that sent me to baptize with water, the Same said unto me, Upon whom thou shalt see the Spirit descending, and remaining on Him, the same is He which baptizeth with the Holy Ghost." (John 1:32-33) The ministry of the Holy Ghost is to guide us into all truth, to show us things to come, and to glorify Jesus. Therefore, it is imperative that we **"GET ANCHORED IN THE TRUTH AND STAND ON HIM,"** because our "Adversary the devil, as a roaring lion, walketh about, seeking whom he may devour," according to I Peter 5:8. We are living in a time wherein evil and wickedness are greatly increased; people are being deceived, and they are deceived by others. Then, the deceived distort the unadulterated Word of God and the life of Jesus, our Lord. We must remember the true doctrine that we have received; Jesus is the personification of that true doctrine.

If you are unsure of what is truth, and you find that you are tossed to and fro with all manner of teachings, here are some things that you can do to **"GET ANCHORED IN THE TRUTH AND STAND ON HIM."**

1. **GET ANCHORED - accept that the Word of God is truth.** Jesus prayed to His Father on behalf of His disciples, "Sanctify them through thy truth: thy word is truth. All Scripture is given by inspiration of God, and is profitable for doctrine, for reproof, for correction, for instruction in righteousness: That the man of God may be perfect, thoroughly furnished unto all good works." (John 17:17; 2 Timothy 3:16-17)

2. **GET ANCHORED – develop a personal relationship with Jesus.** Jesus was the Word that was made flesh [human]. When you are anchored in the Word of God, you are also anchored in Jesus. "And the Word was made flesh, and dwelt among us...." (John 1:14)

3. **GET ANCHORED – be baptized with the Holy Ghost and endued with His power.** John the Baptist told his followers in Luke 3:16 that one would come who would be greater than he, and that He would baptize them with the Holy Ghost and with fire. Jesus told His followers "And, behold, I send the promise of my Father upon you: but tarry ye in the city of Jerusalem, until ye be endued with power from on high." (Luke 24:49)

4. **GET ANCHORED – study the Word of God.** Each one of us is compelled in 2 Timothy 2:15 to "Study to shew thyself approved unto God, a workman that needeth not to be ashamed, rightly dividing the word of truth."

5. **GET ANCHORED – avoid irreverent worthless talk.** This manner of speaking is said to lead to an increase in ungodliness and cause you to err in your faith and life-living. The Word of God cautions us "But shun profane and vain babblings: for they will increase unto more ungodliness." (2 Timothy 2:16)

6. **GET ANCHORED - hide the Word in your heart and let it be your GPS.** The Psalmist wrote "Thy word have I hid in mine heart, that I might not sin against thee. Blessed art thou, O LORD: teach me thy statutes. Thy Word is a lamp unto my feet, and a light unto my path." (Psalm 119:11-12, 105)

AND THEN,

1. **STAND ON HIM – do with confidence and great conviction that which the Word of God says.** "My sheep hear my voice, and I know them, and they follow me: And I give unto them eternal life; and they shall never perish, neither shall any man pluck them out of my hand." (John 10:27-28)

2. **STAND ON HIM – and be light in the midst of darkness.** "Ye are the light of the world. A city that is set on an hill cannot be hid. Let your light so shine before men, that they may see your good works, and glorify your Father which is in heaven." (Matthew 5:14, 16)

CONCLUSION

The Word of God is the anchor that keeps us steadfast in the will and ways of our Lord God. Jesus is the Word in whom we can safely abide. The more we learn about Jesus, the more we should strive to be like Him in this life. This is God's will and purpose for our lives. "For whom He did foreknow, He also did predestinate to be conformed to the image of His Son, that He might be the firstborn among many brethren." (Romans 8:29) Therefore, **"GET ANCHORED IN THE TRUTH AND STAND ON HIM."**

"LIFE THROUGH GOD'S EYES"

Text: **Isaiah 55:8-9** – "For my thoughts are not your thoughts, neither are your ways my ways, saith the Lord. For as the heavens are higher than the earth, so are my ways higher than your ways, and my thoughts than your thoughts."

INTRODUCTION

God's ways are so much higher than our ways. His standards are also higher than any standards that we may set for ourselves. Therefore, if we are to please God, we must see "Life Through God's Eyes." This reality is significant, because we only benefit when our lives are in sync with God's will and His ways. Taking actions and making decisions based on our own thoughts can be detrimental to our eternal destination. This lesson is to caution us to adjust our mindset to think as God thinks and to do as God does, according to the written Word of God He has given to us that we may be able to see **"Life Through God's Eyes."**

DISCUSSION

God is very clear regarding His sovereign power over all of us. He lets us know that there is none like Him, except His only begotten Son and the Holy Spirit of God. These are like Him in His nature and attributes. God makes this fact known through Paul's epistle to the Corinthians, as God explains the details of bodily resurrection. He lets us know that Jesus will successfully make null and void all earthly powers, authorities, regulations, and enemies. Death will be the final enemy that shall be destroyed. God, then, makes a clarification of all that He has previously said, because He wants us to understand that He alone is the One who is in charge of these and all other events in heaven and in earth. God acknowledged that He put all things under the feet of Jesus, but that He, the Father, is not included in those things under Jesus' feet. And, that after Jesus has completed His work, Jesus, Himself, shall also be subject to God, the Father "that God may be all in all." (I Corinthians 15: 28) This is **"Life Through God's Eyes."**

The Word of God is God's written revelation of Himself to us. We are able to know God and what He requires of us through the study of the Holy Scriptures and illuminations that may be revealed to us by the Holy Spirit of God. Therefore, we have no legitimate excuse for disobeying God's instructions to us regarding righteous living for these are clearly noted for us in the Bible. In it, God speaks to all who pick it up and to read it. The full understanding, however, is not readily available to those who have not been born again and have not the Spirit of God dwelling in them. Listed below are some ways we can see **"Life Through God's Eyes."**

1. **Love God with all of our being and our neighbor as we love ourselves.** A lawyer tried to tempt Jesus by asking Him which of the commandments of the law was the greatest. Jesus replied, "Thou shalt love the Lord thy God with all thy heart, and with all thy soul, and with

all thy mind. This is the first and great commandment. And the second is like unto it, Thou shalt love thy neighbor as thyself. On these two commandments hang all the law and the prophets." (Matthew 22:37-40)

2. **Realize that God sent His Son to call sinners to repentance**. The Pharisees questioned why Jesus went to a tax collector's house, and sat and ate with him and other publicans and sinners. Jesus replied, "They that be whole need not a physician, but they that are sick. But go ye and learn what that meaneth, I will have mercy, and not sacrifice: for I am not come to call the righteous, but sinners to repentance." (Matthew 9:12-13)

3. **Believe that Jesus was God's true bread from heaven**. The Lord God fed Israel in the wilderness with bread from heaven, which was called manna, when they were hungry. But, the Father gave them the true bread from heaven, "For the bread of God is He which cometh down from heaven, and giveth life unto the world." (John 6:33) Then said they unto Him, Lord, evermore give us this bread. And Jesus said unto them, "I am the bread of life: he that cometh to Me shall never hunger, and he that believeth on Me shall never thirst." (John 6:35)

4. **Live according to the Word of God.** Satan tempted Jesus in the wilderness and said unto Him, when Satan knew that Jesus was hungry, "If thou be the Son of God, command that these stones be made bread." (Matthew 4:3) Jesus responded, "It is written, Man shall not live by bread alone, but by every word that proceedeth out of the mouth of God." (Matthew 4:4)

5. **Accept that Jesus came down from heaven to do His Father's will.** Jesus gave testimony of Himself. He said, "For I came down from heaven, not to do mine own will, but the will of Him that sent Me. And this is the Father's will which hath sent Me, that of all which He hath given Me I should lose nothing, but should raise it up again at the last day. And this is the will of Him that sent Me, that every one which seeth the Son, and believeth on Him, may have everlasting life: and I will raise him up at the last day." (John 6:38-40)

6. **God must be worshipped in Spirit and in truth.** Our worship must be real, and it should be a reflection of our inner reverence of God for "God is Spirit: and they that worship Him must worship Him in spirit and in truth." (John 4:24)

7. **Jesus is the Way. Follow Him.** Not all ways lead to eternal life. Therefore, we must be careful to choose the right way, because "There is a way which seemeth right unto a man, but the end thereof are the ways of death." (Proverbs 14:12) Jesus said, "Enter ye in at the strait gate: for wide is the gate, and broad is the way, that leadeth to destruction, and many there be which go in thereat: Because strait is the gate, and narrow is the way, which leadeth unto life, and few there be that find it." (Matthew 7:13-14)

8. **Neither words, nor works alone will get you into the Kingdom of God**. Do not depend on your great works and the miracles that you have performed on God's behalf, because Jesus said, "Not every one that saith unto me, Lord, Lord, shall enter into the kingdom of heaven; but he that doeth the will of my Father which is in heaven." (Matthew 7:21)

CONCLUSION

In conclusion, let us end this lesson with a prayer. Lord God, help us to see life through Your eyes and to acknowledge You in all our ways. Direct the paths that we choose, for there is no power in our own wisdom. Clothe us with humility and obedience to Your will and to Your ways.

"MISPLACED AFFECTION"

Text: **Colossians 3:2** – "If ye then be risen with Christ, seek those things which are above, where Christ sitteth on the right hand of God. Set your affection on things above, not on things on the earth."

INTRODUCTION

Those of us who have accepted the Lord Jesus as our Lord and Savior should now view life through new lenses and with new priorities. Each one of us should have come to realize that life is no longer all about self, but it is about allowing Jesus to live through us that He might break our selfish wills, and begin to make us, to shape us, and to mold us into the vessels of honor that He desires us to be. Therefore, our will and our ways should no longer be mainly focused on what we have, or the things of this world that we yet desire, or on all that we have been able to accomplish and accumulate in this world. But, our heart, mind, and life should now be refocused on loving Christ, on pleasing Him by doing His will, and on allowing Him to take us to the place that He desires us to be. Unfortunately, many of us have not made these changes, and therefore, we struggle with **"Misplaced Affection."**

DISCUSSION

This world is not the permanent home of the saved and the unsaved. Therefore, all that we do and hope for must not be set on the things of this world. But we should, rather, do as our lead Scripture says, "Set your affection on things above, not on things on the earth." This mindset will assist us in anchoring ourselves to the proper object of our affection who is Christ Jesus.

In Colossians 3:2, Paul gives us a picture of the life of a true believer by setting forth the principle by which we should live. He begins his writing with a principle that can set us on the right path, as we begin new life with Christ. He suggests that to seek the things on the earth and not those things that are above would be **"Misplaced Affection."** Paul is not

suggesting that we should not have goals and desires for a comfortable life while on the earth. However, he wants us to understand that we should first seek to please God by aligning our priorities with God's priorities. Jesus made this principle very clear in Matthew 6:33, which says, "But seek ye first the kingdom of God, and His righteousness, and all these things shall be added unto you." Therefore, we are to seek first those things and ways that will gain us entrance into the kingdom of God, and apply His principles of holy living in our daily lives. Our hearts' desire is not to build mansions and to accumulate great possessions on the earth, but it is to please Jesus. Seeking the former at the expense of the latter represents **"Misplaced Affection."**

Other examples of **"Misplaced Affection"** are noted below.

1. **Celebrating Christmas as a secular holiday**. It has been a tradition in this country to celebrate December 25th as Christmas in celebration of the birth of Jesus, the Lord and Savior of the world. In the past, both believers and non-believers have participated in this celebration. Over time, this nation has drawn back from celebrating this holiday as the celebration of the birth of Jesus, the Christ. Instead, it is now celebrated as a secular holiday, and Jesus has been removed from national, state, and local celebrations of the holiday. It has become a time to purchase and to exchange gifts with those whom you love; a time for family gatherings and great meals; and a time for travel. The **"Misplaced Affection"** of many believers is seen in their conformity to these new worldviews by focusing on the gift-giving more than on Christ Jesus and His First Coming to save us from our sins; by purchasing and distributing cards that do not celebrate Jesus and the purpose of His coming; and by drawing back from boldly making it known that our celebration is all about Jesus. (See Luke 2:1-40)

2. **Putting all hope of personal, professional, and economic gain in education and the favor or men.** Some of us spend an inordinate amount of time and great effort in seeking degrees and high-paying positions to guarantee that we will be able to purchase a beautiful home and fine clothes; to travel; and to live lavishly in this present world. There is no controversy against having these desires, but the controversy arises when we pursue these only for selfish gain and recognition and without care and concern for those who are in need. (Proverbs 11:4-8; Luke 16:19-31, 12:16-21; Matthew 6:20.) This is **"Misplaced Affection."**

3. **Being attached to that which is temporary**. The things of this world are temporary. To do that which God desires is eternally beneficial to us. We have "Misplaced Affection" when we are too attached to that which is temporary. (Matthew 6:19-21)

4. **Using the standards of this world to order our lives.** Our affection is misplaced when we love that which the world loves; we adopt that which the world says is acceptable; and when we measure the things of God by the standards of the world. (Romans 12:1-2; Isaiah 5:20; John 17:17; Hebrews 4:12)

5. **Thinking on the wrong things**. The Apostle Paul tells us in I Corinthians 6:12 that "All things are lawful unto me, but all things are not expedient: all things are lawful for me, but I will not be brought under the power of any." If we are "brought under the power of" things of this world, our affections will be misplaced. Philippians 4:8-9 tells us how to protect ourselves from **"Misplaced Affection."** We are told "... Whatsoever things are true, whatsoever things are honest, whatsoever things are just, whatsoever things are pure, whatsoever things are lovely, whatsoever things are of good report; if there be any virtue, and if there be any praise, think on these things." (I Corinthians 6:12; Philippians 4:8-9)

CONCLUSION

In conclusion, as true believers we should take time to evaluate the focus of our affection. It is clear that the affection of true believers should be on things above, and not on things in the earth. Finally, we should realize that a change of heart leads to a change of thoughts. A change of thoughts lead to a change of affection. **LET YOUR AFFECTION BE ON JESUS!**

"OUR WORDS MATTER"

Text: **Matthew 12:36-37** – "But I say unto you, that every idle word that men shall speak, they shall give account thereof in the day of judgment. For by thy words thou shalt be justified, and by thy words thou shalt be condemned."

INTRODUCTION

In every civilization, people use words to communicate with each other in various ways. Words may be used to build up, or to tear down a person's self-esteem; to express one's ideas and thoughts; and to encourage, or to discourage another, etc. The energy, sound, and frequency of our words have great power. Therefore, we should be careful of the words that we speak to each other, the tone that we use when speaking, and the methods we choose to deliver our words, because **"Our Words Matter."**

DISCUSSION

Words are our most commonly used means of communicating with each other. These speech tones, both written and verbal, can tear down or build up; encourage or discourage; make happy or make sad. Words can do great damage or much good in another's life and in the Body of Christ. Once hurtful words are spoken, others may forgive us, and we may be very sorry for that which we have spoken, but the power and effect of those words cannot be withdrawn from the ears, minds, and hearts of those who heard them.

The Word of God tells us that words reflect the things that are in a person's heart. Jesus said, "A good man out of the good treasure of the heart bringeth forth good things: and an evil man out of the evil treasure bringeth forth evil things." (Matthew 12:35) James, the step-brother of our Lord Jesus Christ, asks a question in the epistle that also carries his name, verse 11. He asked, "Doth a fountain send forth at the same place sweet water and bitter?" He wanted Jewish believers to whom the epistle was written, and believers today to realize and accept that words reflect our true identity. Therefore, we should be careful to think before we speak. James outlined this principle in chapter one, verse nineteen of his epistle in which he wrote, "Wherefore, my beloved brethren, let every man be swift to hear, slow to speak, slow to wrath:" The swift speaking of two biblical characters caused them great grief and regret. **"Our Words Matter."**

It is good when our words and our promises line up with our actions. However, we should also be careful to consider all of the possible consequences that may result from the words that we speak and the promises that we make, because **"Our Words Matter."** The swift speaking of two biblical characters caused them great grief and regret. I am reminded of an unnecessarily hasty and ridiculous vow that was made by a man named Jephthah. "And Jephthah vowed a vow unto the LORD, and said, If thou shalt without fail deliver the children of Ammon into mine hands, then it shall be, that whatsoever cometh forth of the doors of my house to meet me, when I return in peace from the children of Ammon, shall surely be the LORD's, and I will offer it up for a burnt offering." God gave Jephthah the victory, but on his return his only daughter and child came out to meet him. Needless to say, Jephthah was very sorrowful, but he kept his word, and he offered up his daughter. It was not a requirement that Jephthah make such a vow. He spoke too quickly, without considering the possible consequences of such a vow. He kept his words, but he lost his daughter. Another example of speaking too quickly is when Herod promised Salome "with an oath to give her whatsoever she would ask." (Matthew 14:7)

She asked for the head of John the Baptist in a charger [on a platter]. Herod was sorrowful, but he kept his oath.

Listed below are other reasons why **"Our Words Matter."**

1. **Your words can kill**. "Death and life are in the power of the tongue: and they that love it shall eat the fruit thereof." (Proverbs 18:21) Your words have consequences, and you will reap whatsoever you sow.

2. **You will be held accountable for your words**. "...every idle word that men shall speak, they shall give account thereof in the day of judgment. For by thy words thou shalt be justified, and by thy words thou shall be condemned." (Matthew 12:36-37)

3. **The Word of God can be a weapon.** "For the Word of God is quick, and powerful, and sharper than any two-edged sword, piercing even to the dividing asunder of soul and spirit, and of the joints and marrow, and is a discerner of the thoughts and intents of the heart." (Hebrews 4:12)

4. **Your words can keep you out of trouble**. "Whoso keepeth his mouth and his tongue keepeth his soul from troubles, and He that keepeth his mouth keepeth his life: but he that openeth wide his lips shall have destruction." (Proverbs 21:23; 13:3)

5. **Words can be indicators of your salvation**. "If any man among you seem to be religious, and bridleth not his tongue, but deceiveth his own heart, this man's religion is vain." (James 1:26)

6. **Words reveal your heart**. "But those things which proceed out of the mouth come forth from the heart, and they defile the man. For out of the heart proceed evil thoughts, murders, adulteries, fornications, thefts, false witness, blasphemies." (Matthew 15:18-19)

7. **Words can change a life**. Tell somebody, "For God so loved the world, that He gave His only begotten Son, that whosoever believeth in Him should not perish, but have everlasting life. For God sent not His Son into the world to condemn the world; but that the world through Him might be saved." (John 3:16-17)

CONCLUSION

Therefore, be careful of the words you speak, how you speak them, and to whom they are spoken. **"Our Words Matter."**

"A GRATEFUL HEART"

Text: **Luke 17:15-16** - "And one of them, when he saw that he was healed, turned back, and with a loud voice glorified God, And fell down on his face at His feet, giving Him thanks: and he was a Samaritan."

INTRODUCTION

The scriptural texts for this lesson begin with a phrase that lets us know that there must have been more than one person involved in this particular event. The words of the second phrase tell us that the main character was a male, and that he had some type of disease. Other portions of the narrative tell us that as he went, as he was instructed, he realized that he was healed. The joy of his healing brought about praise in his heart. And, we are told that he glorified God with a loud voice of thanks and with humility.

DISCUSSION

God is a good God! He has done so many wonderful things for each of us in our lives. How many times has God brought you through grave financial situations, e.g., some could have been evicted from your home or apartment; some could have had a car repossessed; some could be dead and in the grave; some could be gravely sick unto death; etc. Gratefully, we made it through the situation. It is sad to say, however, many of us did not give God glory and thanks for these victories that only He could have turned those situations in our favor. We should be careful to not take God for granted; with God, there are no entitlements.

The man in our text was one of ten lepers, who resided in a village in Samaria. Jesus traveled through Samaria on His way to Galilee, where lepers were confined to their own village. They were forbidden to be among the masses, without first alerting them of their approach. The system for the verification of cleanliness from leprosy required that the leper go to the priest for certification that one was, indeed, cleansed from this disease. Jesus healed ten, but only one of them returned to say "Thank you." Have you told God thanks for the blessings that He has bestowed upon you and your family?

The word "heart" refers both to the physical organ and to the spiritual center of our being. Physically, it is a muscular organ that pumps blood throughout the body's circulatory system by movements of contraction and dilation. Spiritually, the heart is the immaterial center of a person's character. The Word of God tells us in Luke 6:45 that "A good man out of the good treasure of his heart bringeth forth that which is good; and an evil man out of the evil treasure of his heart bringeth forth that which is evil: for of the abundance of the heart his mouth speaketh." Therefore, "Keep thy heart with all diligence; for out of it are the issues of life," according to Proverbs 4:23.

Do you have a grateful heart? Let us observe a few examples in the Word of God of "A Grateful Heart."

1. **A Grateful Heart** acknowledges God's blessings and keeps the promises that were made in the original petition to God. Hannah was barren, and she was tormented by her husband's other wife, Peninnah. Hannah prayed to God to give her a son. She promised the Lord God that she would give her son to Him all the days of his life. God honored her prayer, and she was grateful. She told Eli, the priest, "Oh my lord as thy soul liveth, my lord, I am the woman that stood by thee here, praying unto the LORD. For this child I prayed; and the LORD hath given me my petition which I asked of Him: Therefore also I have lent him to the LORD; as long as he liveth he shall be lent to the LORD. And he worshipped the LORD there." (I Samuel 1:26-28)

2. **A Grateful Heart** loves God as the Holy Scriptures command, and that love for God causes a grateful heart to strive to keep God's commandments. Mark 12:30 says, "And thou shalt love the Lord thy God with all thy heart, and with all thy soul, and with all thy mind, and with all thy strength: this is the first commandment." John 14:15 says, "If ye love Me, keep My commandments."

3. **A Grateful Heart** leaves the unthankful group and returns to glorify God. "And when He saw them, He said unto them, Go shew yourselves unto the priests. And it came to pass, that, as they went, they were cleansed. And one of them, when he saw that he was healed, turned back and with a loud voice glorified God, And fell down on his face at His feet, giving Him thanks: and he was a Samaritan." (Luke 17:14-16)

4. **A Grateful Heart** is a living witness of God's power and His favor. Before Jesus raised Lazarus from the dead, He openly prayed to His Father, so that the people who stood by might believe. "Then they took away the stone from the place where the dead was laid. And Jesus lifted up His eyes, and said, Father, I thank thee that thou hast heard me. And I knew that thou hearest me always: but because of the people which stand by I said it, that they may believe that thou hast sent me." (John 11:41-42)

5. **A Grateful Heart** realizes that God only is the deliverer. "Know ye not that the unrighteous shall not inherit the kingdom of God? Be not deceived: neither fornicators, nor idolaters, nor adulterers, nor effeminate, nor abusers of themselves with mankind, Nor thieves, nor covetous, nor drunkards, nor revilers, nor extortioners, shall inherit the kingdom of God. And such were some of you: but ye are washed, but ye are sanctified, but ye are justified in the name of the Lord Jesus, and by the Spirit of our God." (I Corinthians 6:9-11)

6. **A Grateful Heart** does not fear in times of testing, but it leans on the biblical principle that says, "My brethren, count it all joy when ye fall into divers temptations; Knowing this, that the trying of your faith worketh patience. But let patience have her perfect work, that ye may be perfect and entire, wanting nothing." (James 1:2-4)

CONCLUSION

Lord, give us a **"Grateful Heart"** for all that you have done for us, in us, and through us. We realize that we can do nothing without you. And so, Lord, in everything we give You thanks. We offer the sacrifice of praise to [You] continually, that is, the fruit of our lips giving thanks to Your name. (I Thessalonians 5:18; Hebrews 13:15)

"LORD, HELP US TO STAND"

Text: Matthew 24:21-22 - "For then shall be great tribulation, such as was not since the beginning of the world to this time, no, nor ever shall be. And except those days should be shortened, there should no flesh be saved: but for the elect's sake those days shall be shortened."

INTRODUCTION

The Holy Scriptures paint a very discouraging and frightening picture of the way things will be in the last days. Our text states that things will be so bad that "for the elect's sake those days shall be shortened." (Matthew 24:22b) The epistle of II Timothy, chapter 3, further describes this time as "perilous," which means "dangerous, unsafe, grievous, treacherous, and unsound" times, according to Merriam-Webster's Dictionary and Thesaurus. And, even though "...all that will live godly in Christ Jesus shall suffer persecution" (II Timothy 3:12), Lord, Help *Us* to Stand and to heed the instruction that the Apostle Paul gave to Timothy, which was to "...continue thou in the things which thou hast learned and hast been assured of, knowing of whom thou hast learned them."

DISCUSSION

We are living in a time of great apathy towards God and our fellow men and women. People are intolerant, blatantly disrespectful towards one another, selfish, without compassion and totally detached from the cares and concerns of others. These are signs of a nation that is in great spiritual and moral decline. Today, hatred and racial animosity have been normalized as anticipated behaviors, wherein no one is surprised, neither overly concerned about them. These behaviors and attitudes are directly opposite of the behaviors that have been commanded of the children of God. How should the true children of God respond in times like these? We should ask God's help. Ask God to do the following:

1. **Guide our conversations** – "But as He which hath called you is holy, so be ye holy in all manner of conversation." (I Peter 1:15)

2. **Keep our heart** – "...with all diligence; for out of it are the issues of life. A good man out of the good treasure of his heart bringeth forth that which is good; ...for of the abundance of the heart his mouth speaketh." (Proverbs 4:23; Luke 6:45a)

3. **Keep us striving for the gospel** by standing fast in one spirit, with one mind striving together for the faith of the gospel, as noted in Philippians 1:27.

4. **Let our faith stand** – "...not in the wisdom of men, but in the power of God." (1 Corinthians 2:5)

5. **Help us to stand in affliction** – "For our light affliction, which is but for a moment; worketh for us a far more exceeding and eternal weight of glory. For I reckon that the sufferings of this present time are not worthy to be compared with the glory which shall be revealed in us." (2 Corinthians 4:17; Romans 8:18)

6. **Give us humble spirits** that are subject unto Your Holy Spirit. "For they that are after the flesh do mind the things of the flesh; but they that are after the Spirit the things of the Spirit. For to be carnally minded is death; but to be spiritually minded is life and peace. Because the carnal mind is enmity against God: for it is not subject to the law of God, neither indeed can be." (Romans 8:5-7)

CONCLUSION

In these last days, it is critical that we remain steadfast and unmovable in the truth, as outlined in the Word of God, and in the faith that we have received. Many have compromised the ways of God for the pleasures of this world, which lead to spiritual demise.

"Lord, Help Us To Stand." When "We are troubled on every side," let us not be distressed. When "We are perplexed," let us not be in despair. And, though at times we may be "Persecuted," help us to know that we are not forsaken; "Cast down, but not destroyed." (2 Corinthians 4:8-9)

Finally, "Nay, in all these things we are more than conquerors through Him that loved us. For I am persuaded, that neither death, nor life, nor angels, nor principalities, nor powers, nor things present, nor things to come, Nor height, nor depth, nor any other creature, shall be able to separate us from the love of God, which is in Christ Jesus our Lord." (Romans 8:37-39)

Lesson Number Forty

"JESUS: THE BELIEVER'S ROLE MODEL"

Text: Mark 1:12-13 – "And immediately the Spirit driveth Him into the wilderness. And He was there in the wilderness forty days, tempted of Satan; and was with the wild beasts; and the angels ministered unto Him."

INTRODUCTION

In this life, it is not unusual for a believer to be greatly impressed by the gifts, talents, personalities, and achievements of sports figures, actors and actresses, various stage performers, and of the rich and famous. These impressions often lead to the observer's desire to be just like the one that he or she admires. The one who is the object of the imitation is called a "role model." However, oftentimes, a role model disappoints the admirer by making poor life choices, speaking words that may offend, or taking actions that are deemed inappropriate. Needless to say, these shortcomings could cause an admirer to have a change of heart towards the role model. But, there is one role model who will never disappoint His admirers. His name is Jesus.

DISCUSSION

Immediately after John baptized Jesus, the Scripture tells us that Jesus was driven by the Spirit into the wilderness of Judea. The wilderness was a desolate waste and lonely place. This event is also reported in the gospels of Matthew and Luke. However, their accounts more fully detail all that Jesus suffered in the wilderness. Mark's account is a summary of the wilderness experience. He tells us that Jesus was driven into the wilderness by the Spirit; that He was there forty days with the wild beasts being tempted of Satan; and after all of these, the angels came and ministered to Him.

A review of the more detailed accounts of this narrative reveals that Jesus was tempted at all points. Yet, He endured every temptation, and He was victorious over the devil. His example to the believer is that even though life's journey may be filled with various temptations, the Word of God can give a believer the strength to endure. Jesus was the perfect role model for living godly in this present world. The character traits and obedience that Jesus exemplified are worthy of being modeled by the believer when tempted by Satan. Some of these are listed below.

1. **Jesus knew the source of His temptations**. "Get thee hence, Satan...." (Matthew 4:10b). It is important that every believer knows who is their real enemy. The real enemy is not the person who commits an evil act against a believer. Satan is the source of every evil temptation that is planted in the heart and mind of offenders. (Matthew 4:1)

2. **Don't give in to temptations**. Temptations will surely come. However, just know that temptations come to test your obedience to God's will and His ways. Therefore, be on

guard and prepared for testing with the Word of God in your heart and in your mouth. Jesus spoke the Word. You speak the Word, and follow the Role Model.

3. **Stay true to your God-given mission.** God's mission for humankind was delayed, because of the disobedience of Adam and Eve. When they were tested, they failed the test by obeying Satan, rather than God. Jesus, however, who is called the second Adam, endured and overcame His testing that He might fulfill the mission given Him by the Father. That mission was, and is, to be the means of salvation for fallen humankind, who are separated from God their Creator. "For if by one man's offence death reigned by ne; much more they which receive abundance of grace and of the gift of righteousness shall reign in life by one, Jesus Christ." (Romans 5:19) Jesus accomplished His mission. Let us accomplish our mission to win souls (Proverbs 11:30b – "...and he that winneth souls is wise."); and to be light in this dark and evil world and salt to the earth (Matthew 5:13-14), as Jesus instructed. A believer's knowledge of God's Word is necessary, but it is without effect in the believer's life when the believer disobeys it (James 1:22). Jesus obeyed the Word, therefore we should obey the Word, and follow the Role Model.

4. **Don't compromise when the journey gets rough**. "And when He had fasted forty days and forty nights, He was afterward an hungred." (Matthew 4:2) We must remember that Jesus was fully human, as we are human. But, even though He was certainly hungry, He did not yield to any of Satan's tactics, e.g., to turn stones into bread (Matthew 4:3-4); or to cast Himself down from the pinnacle of the temple to test the angel's charge concerning Him (4:4-7); neither was Jesus impressed by the glory of the kingdoms of this world, which Satan offered to Him (4:8-10). Jesus did not grow weary in obeying God and in resisting the devil. He made no concessions with Satan to lighten His burdens. Believers should not compromise, when it seems as though all hope is gone. Follow the Role Model.

CONCLUSION

Therefore, let us remember that Jesus is the Way, the Truth, and the Life. He is the believer's role model. If we follow the pattern of life that He has shown us in the Word of God, we, too, shall be victorious both in this life and in the life that is yet to come. "For even hereunto were ye called: because Christ also suffered for us, leaving us an example, that ye should follow His steps: who did not sin, neither was guile found in His mouth:." (I Peter 2:21-22) Follow the Role Model, for that role model is Jesus.

"GOD DELIGHTS IN OBEDIENCE"

Text: **I Samuel 15:22-24** – "And Samuel said, Hath the Lord as great delight in burnt offerings and sacrifices, as in obeying the voice of the Lord? Behold, to obey is better than sacrifice, and to hearken than the fat of rams."

INTRODUCTION

The narrative behind this text is an excellent example of an old adage which says, "The end does not justify the means." Both the text and the adage suggest that doing that which God has commanded is more important to God than that which may be offered, or gained by disobedience to God's commands. We deceive our own selves, when we are swayed by our perceptions of that which God has commanded, and/or by projections of benefits that might be derived from a slight alteration of God's plans.

DISCUSSION

A review of the circumstances that pertain to the text for this lesson explicitly depicts the sovereignty of God. The word "sovereignty" means "Supreme power or authority; self-governance; self-rule; and self-determination," according to a Google search of the word. These suggest that supreme power is not accountable to any one, neither is it accountable to any other rule, power, or dominion. In other words, it is God's innate right to decide and to execute His will and purposes in heaven and in earth regarding situations and persons. Whatever God does is right, because He is the standard by which He is judged. God's commands are righteous, and they are rooted in justice and wisdom. God reminds us in the Holy Scriptures that "...My thoughts are not your thoughts, neither are your ways My ways, saith the Lord. For as the heavens are higher than the earth, so are my ways higher than your ways, and my thoughts than your thoughts." (Isaiah 55:8-9). Therefore, we should take care in judging God's instructions to King Saul, God's displeasure regarding Saul's disobedience, and the penalties that God imposed upon Saul.

When the Lord God sent the prophet Samuel to anoint Saul as king, He also sent a message to him, with specific instructions that he should perform against Amalek, the nation of the grandson of Esau, son of Isaac and Rebekah, which also bear his name. Amalek cowardly attacked Israel's rear ranks, who were tired and weary and lagged behind the main army after they were delivered through the Red Sea. The Lord God promised to never forget what Amalek did, and to utterly destroy them for their act. (Deuteronomy 25:17-18) Saul either forgot what the descendants of Amalek did to Israel, or he chose to ignore it. But, God neither forgot that which Amalek had done, neither did He ignore it. His instructions to Saul were given with God's ultimate plan in mind to wipe the presence and even the remembrance of Amalek and his descendants from the face of the earth. Saul's explanations for disobeying God were met by Samuel's strong question to Saul. He asked Saul, "Hath the Lord as great delight in burnt-offerings and sacrifices, as in obeying the voice of the Lord?" (I Samuel

15:22) Samuel answered his own question, and he told Saul, "Behold, to obey is better than sacrifice, and to hearken than the fat of rams." (I Samuel 15:22)

The following principles are observed from this lesson.

1. **Offerings and sacrifices are not sufficient to explain away disobedience.** "For I spake not unto your fathers, nor commanded them in the day that I brought them out of the land of Egypt, concerning burnt-offerings or sacrifices: But this thing commanded I them, saying, Obey My voice, and I will be your God, and ye shall be My people: and walk ye in all the ways that I have commanded you, that it may be well unto you." (Jeremiah 7:22-23)

2. **God remembers His promise.** "Remember what Amalek did unto thee by the way, when ye were come forth out of Egypt; How he met thee by the way, and smote the hindmost of thee, even all that were feeble behind thee, when thou wast faint and weary; and he feared not God. Therefore it shall be, when the Lord thy God hath given thee rest from all thine enemies round about, in the land which the Lord thy God giveth thee for an inheritance to possess it, that thou shalt blot out the remembrance of Amalek from under heaven; thou shalt not forget it." (Deuteronomy 25:17-19) God wanted to accomplish His promise through Saul. But, Saul was not willing to obey God.

3. **Oftentimes, God's ultimate purpose is not made known to us.** God's statements regarding Amalek and his descendants suggest that He was not only concerned about their being a present threat to Israel. God wanted to prevent Amalek from ever again being a threat to His people. Saul's failure to "utterly destroy" Amalek and his descendants, as God instructed, allowed the Amalekites to remain as thorns in Israel's side from generation to generation. During the reign of King Ahasuerus of Persia, Haman, an Amalekite in the palace of the king, sought to have the Hebrew nation destroyed. But, God planted Esther, a beautiful Hebrew girl, in the palace of the king. God used her to prevent the destruction of her people, and Haman was put to death.

4. **Partial obedience to God's commands is unacceptable.** When Saul was confronted by Samuel regarding his disobedience to God's commands, Saul responded, "Yea, I have obeyed the voice of the Lord, and have gone the way which the Lord sent me, and have brought Agag the king of Amalek, and have utterly destroyed the Amalekites. But the people took of the spoil, sheep, and the oxen, the chief of the things which should have been utterly destroyed, to sacrifice unto the Lord thy God in Gilgal." (I Samuel 15:20-21)

5. Instead of destroying all of these, as God had instructed, the people and Saul revised God's instructions to sacrifice unto Him. God's response through Samuel was "Behold, to obey is better than sacrifice, and to hearken than the fat of rams." (I Samuel 15:22)

CONCLUSION

Full obedience to God's commands is required by God. We cannot pick and choose which commands we will obey, and which commands we will disobey. The key principle that we should remember in this lesson is that **"God Delights in Obedience,"** more than the offerings that we might give, or the gifts and talents that we might offer in service to Him.

"THE JOB MENTALITY"

Text: **Job 1:20** – "Then Job arose, and rent his mantle, and shaved his head, and feel down upon the ground, and worshipped, and said, Naked came I out of my mother's womb, and naked shall I return thither: the Lord gave, and the Lord hath taken away; blessed be the name of the Lord. In all this Job sinned not, nor charged God foolishly."

INTRODUCTION

It is a natural propensity for us to be disheartened when terrible things happen to us in this life. If we are truthful, it is highly unlikely that many of us will feel like worshipping God in the midst of trials and tribulations. Job, the main character in this narrative, is described by the text as a man who "Was perfect and upright, and one that feared God, and eschewed evil." (Job 1:1b) These words "feared God" do not mean that Job was afraid of God; they mean that Job held God in high esteem. He reverenced God. The words "eschewed evil" simply mean that Job consciously and deliberately avoided evil. In all of Job's calamities, his faith and obedience were greatly tested.

DISCUSSION

Job, a man of great wealth and possessions, seven sons and three daughters, lost everything in the space of one day. In a series of losses throughout the day, Job received message after message that his oxen and asses were stolen and his servants were slain; that his sheep and servants were burned up by fire that fell down from heaven; that his camels were taken and his servants killed, "and finally, that a great wind from the wilderness smote the house wherein his seven sons and three daughters were visiting and celebrating with each other, and all of them were killed, when the house collapsed upon them. Just reading the Scriptural presentations of these calamities were overwhelming and painful. While one of his servants was telling Job about his oxen and asses, another servant interrupted them with news that his sheep and servants were consumed by fire. Before that servant could finish speaking, another servant came in to tell Job that his camels had been taken and his servants were killed. And, while that servant was speaking, another servant entered to tell him that all of his children were dead.

Many of us would have lost our mind. Or, we would have become very angry with God. Job did neither of these. Let us consider what I call **"The Job Mentality,"** which summarizes Job's responses to the dilemmas that he faced.

1. **Job acknowledged God's sovereign authority** over everything God had given to him. "Naked came I out of my mother's womb, and naked shall I return thither: the Lord gave, and the Lord hath taken away; blessed be the name of the Lord." (Job 1:21)

2. **God is worthy of praise in times of suffering and blessing.** "Then said his wife unto him, Dost thou still retain thine integrity? curse God, and die. But he said unto her, Thou speakest as one of the foolish women speaketh. What? shall we receive good at

the hand of God, and shall we not receive evil? In all this did not Job sin with his lips." (Job 2:9-10)

3. **Job worshipped God even after he had lost everything.** "Then Job arose, and rent his mantle, and shaved his head, and fell down upon the ground, and worshipped...." (Job 1:20)

4. **Job remained faithful to God and his faith in God never waivered.** "In all this Job sinned not, nor charged God foolishly." (Job 1:22)

5. **Job loved and respected God, and kept himself from evil.** "And the Lord said unto Satan, Hast thou considered my servant Job, that there is none like him in the earth, a perfect and an upright man, one that feareth God, and escheweth evil? (Job 1:8)

6. **Job loved God when he was blessed and when he was suffering.** "But He knoweth the way that I take: when He hath tried me, I shall come forth as gold. My foot hath held His steps, His way have I kept, and not declined. (Job 23:10-11)

7. **Job accepted what God allowed in his life and remained faithful.** "And now, Lord, what wait I for? my hope is in thee." (Psalm 39:7)

8. **Job's life was built on God and not on material possessions.** When everything Job had was gone, he still had God.

CONCLUSION

In conclusion, **"The Job Mentality"** simply shows us how we might respond during our times of testing. The most important point in Job's responses to his situation is that we must never lose faith in God. He is our anchor. He is our strength. He is our hope. And, with Him all things are possible. Job held on to God, and ..."the LORD blessed the latter end of Job more than his beginning: for he had fourteen thousand sheep, and six thousand camels, and a thousand yoke of oxen, and a thousand she asses. He had also seven sons and three daughters." (Job 42:12-13). God greatly rewards those who are faithful to the end.

Lesson Number Forty-Three

"FAITH THAT IS REAL: DO YOU HAVE IT?"

Text: **Matthew 8:5-8** – "And when Jesus was entered into Capernaum, there came unto Him a centurion, beseeching Him, and saying, Lord, my servant lieth at home sick of the palsy, grievously tormented. And Jesus saith unto him, I will come and heal him. The centurion answered and said, Lord, I am not worthy that thou shouldest come under my roof: but speak the word only, and my servant shall be healed."

INTRODUCTION

Many of us profess that we have faith. And, generally speaking this is a true statement, for the Word of God tells us in Romans 12:3 that God has given all of humankind "the measure of faith." This measure of faith is needed to peaceably and confidently live in this world, as we go about our daily living. This basic measure of faith allows us to accomplish our daily tasks with confidence. For an example, we do not test every chair before we sit in it to determine whether or not it will successfully hold our weight. We put our hard-earned money into banks, with faith that it will be safely kept and made available to us when we desire to access it. It takes this same basic faith to receive salvation that is firmly rooted in Christ Jesus. But, "Faith That Is Real" is not static, neither is it passive; it is active and alive. "Faith That Is Real" is a faith that automatically works, as a result of our profession of that faith. Also, it is displayed to the world as real by the combination of its profession and its works.

DISCUSSION

The Word of God describes faith as, "The substance of things hoped for, the evidence of things not seen." (Hebrews 11:1) The doctrine of faith identifies the substance of a thing as that which is hidden in time and space, but is brought forth into the visible realm by our confidence and trust in the person of Jesus, His written word, and His miraculous power. This confidence and trust give us the mind and strength to patiently wait with expectation for the visible manifestation of the thing for which we hope. As we wait, "Faith That Is Real," does not doubt that the thing shall surely come to pass. The question is, "Do You Have It?"

The centurion, an officer of the Roman army, came to Jesus on behalf of his servant who was at home in great pain. When Jesus offered to come home with him, the centurion counted himself unworthy of Jesus's presence in his home. His faith in the person of Jesus, and in the great powers that Jesus displayed throughout the region, led the centurion to believe that if Jesus would only speak healing words on behalf of his servant that his servant would, indeed, be healed. And, the Word of God reports that the servant was healed around the same time that Jesus spoke the words of healing.

Examine your faith by the following principles of a "Faith That Is Real."

1. **Faith that is real is fully-persuaded** that what we desire shall surely come to pass. It rejects all tendencies to doubt what God has promised. God cannot lie. Whatsoever He has promised, we must be fully convinced that He will do. "Verily, verily, I say unto you, He that believeth on Me, the works that I do shall he do also; and greater works than these shall he do; because I go unto My Father. And whatsoever ye shall ask in My name, that will I do, that the Father may be glorified in the Son. If ye shall ask any thing in My name, I will do it." (John 14:12-14)

2. **Faith that is real withstands adversity.** Joseph dreamed a dream, and he told it to his father, mother, and brothers. The dream revealed that Joseph would reign over all of them. Joseph's brothers hated him even the more for this dream, and his father rebuked him. (Genesis 37:5, 10) Through all that Joseph suffered, he never waivered in that which God showed to him in a dream.

3. **Faith that is real endures when it is tried and tested**. God allowed Satan to test His servant, Job. Job lost all of his possessions and his family, but Job yet loved and trusted God. His faith was real, for it was rooted in God. (Job 1: 13-22; 42:12-13)

4. **Faith that is real is not based on situations and circumstances**. In this life, it is a known fact that we will have trials and tribulations. Nevertheless, we should not lose faith, nor waiver in our faith. Three Hebrew boys were among those who were taken into Babylonian captivity. But, when their faith in the teachings they had received was tested, they refused to compromise. "Shadrach, Meshach, and Abed-nego, answered and said to the king, O Nebuchadnezzar, we are not careful to answer thee in this matter. If it be so, our God whom we serve is able to deliver us from the burning fiery furnace, and He will deliver us out of thine hand, O king. But if not, be it known unto thee, O king, that we will not serve thy gods, nor worship the golden image which thou hast set up." (Daniel 3:16-18)

5. **Faith that is real makes the impossible thing possible**. God chose a virgin to bring our Lord and Savior into the world. We know that in the natural, it is impossible for a woman to have a baby and still be a bonafide virgin. Yet, faith that is real believes what the Holy Word of God says: "Joseph, thou son of David, fear not to take unto thee Mary thy wife: for that which is conceived in her is of the Holy Ghost. And she shall bring forth a son, and thou shalt call his name JESUS. Then Joseph being raised from sleep did as the angel of the Lord had bidden him, and took unto him his wife: And knew her not till she had brought forth her firstborn son: and he called his name JESUS." (Matthew 1:20, 21, 24, 25) Real faith believes that "With God nothing shall be impossible." (Luke 1:37) Faith that is real makes us available to God to be used by Him to accomplish the impossible.

CONCLUSION

In conclusion, let us examine our faith to determine whether it is real. Does it meet the criteria discussed in this lesson? Or, is it a faith that is filled with doubt, fear, and inconsistencies that rely on life's circumstances? Finally, let us submit ourselves to God for His examination, and invite Him to strengthen our faith, if it is not real. We can build our faith by reading and listening to God's Word and "hearing" it deep in our spirit. "... Faith cometh by hearing, and hearing by the Word of God." (Romans 10:17)